Lecture Notes in Artificial Intelligence 12947

Subseries of Lecture Notes in Computer Science

Series Editors

Randy Goebel
University of Alberta, Edmonton, Canada
Yuzuru Tanaka
Hokkaido University, Sapporo, Japan
Wolfgang Wahlster
DFKI and Saarland University, Saarbrücken, Germany

Founding Editor

Jörg Siekmann
DFKI and Saarland University, Saarbrücken, Germany

Tobias Ahlbrecht · Jürgen Dix ·
Niklas Fiekas · Tabajara Krausburg (Eds.)

The Multi-Agent Programming Contest 2021

One-and-a-Half Decades of Exploring
Multi-Agent Systems

 Springer

Editors
Tobias Ahlbrecht ⓘ
TU Clausthal
Clausthal-Zellerfeld, Germany

Niklas Fiekas ⓘ
TU Clausthal
Clausthal-Zellerfeld, Germany

Jürgen Dix ⓘ
TU Clausthal
Clausthal-Zellerfeld, Germany

Tabajara Krausburg ⓘ
TU Clausthal
Clausthal-Zellerfeld, Germany

PUCRS
Porto Alegre, Brazil

ISSN 0302-9743   ISSN 1611-3349   (electronic)
Lecture Notes in Artificial Intelligence
ISBN 978-3-030-88548-9   ISBN 978-3-030-88549-6   (eBook)
https://doi.org/10.1007/978-3-030-88549-6

LNCS Sublibrary: SL7 – Artificial Intelligence

This Springer imprint is published by the registered company Springer Nature Switzerland AG
The registered company address is: Gewerbestrasse 11, 6330 Cham, Switzerland

Preface

In this volume, we present the fifteenth edition of the annual Multi-Agent Programming Contest.

The first paper gives an overview of the competition, describes the current scenario, summarises this year's participants and their approaches, and analyses some of the matches played and the contest as a whole.

For the second part, each team contributed a paper describing their approach and experiences with creating a team of agents to participate in the contest.

The review process was single blind and on average three reviews were conducted per contribution. Each team was able to pass the review process without problems.

July 2021

Tobias Ahlbrecht
Jürgen Dix
Niklas Fiekas
Tabajara Krausburg

Organization

Program Chairs

Tobias Ahlbrecht   TU Clausthal, Germany
Rem Collier   University College Dublin, Ireland
Jürgen Dix   TU Clausthal, Germany
Niklas Fiekas   TU Clausthal, Germany
Tabajara Krausburg   TU Clausthal, Germany

Program Committee

Lars Braubach   City University of Applied Sciences, Bremen, Germany
Rem Collier   University College Dublin, Ireland
Debora Engelmann   Pontifícia Universidade Católica do Rio Grande do Sul, Brazil
Babak Esfandiari   Carleton University, Canada
Brian Logan   University of Nottingham, UK
Alison Panisson   Federal University of Santa Catarina, Brazil
Alessandro Ricci   University of Bologna, Cesena, Italy
Sebastian Sardina   RMIT University, Australia
Evangelos Sarmas   Independent, Greece
Federico Schlesinger   Zalando SE, Germany
Neil Yorke-Smith   TU Delft, The Netherlands

Contents

Overview

The 15th Multi-Agent Programming Contest
Assemble with Care

Tobias Ahlbrecht[1]([⊠])[iD], Jürgen Dix[1][iD], Niklas Fiekas[1][iD],
and Tabajara Krausburg[1,2][iD]

[1] Department of Informatics, Clausthal University of Technology,
Clausthal-Zellerfeld, Germany
{tobias.ahlbrecht,dix,niklas.fiekas}@tu-clausthal.de
[2] School of Technology, Pontifical Catholic University of Rio Grande do Sul,
Porto Alegre, Brazil
tabajara.rodrigues@edu.pucrs.br

Abstract. The Multi-Agent Programming Contest, MAPC, is an
(almost) annual competition with international participants. The contestants develop a multi-agent system that has to compete against each
other team in a series of games, requiring cooperation, collaboration,
planning capabilities and much more. The contest goals are twofold: We
try to find scenarios, where it pays off to use the tools of agent-oriented
software engineering, and we try to encourage people to learn about or
even refine those tools. We present the contest's 15th edition, its participants and results.

Keywords: multi-agent systems · agent-based simulation ·
decentralized computing · cooperation · artificial intelligence ·
simulation platforms

1 Introduction

Multi-agent systems is a field in Artificial Intelligence that focuses on the cooperation, coordination and social abilities of software entities (hereby called *agents*).
Much work has been done in the last three decades to formally define concepts and their relationships to express the behavior of agents; in particular
autonomous agents. As an example, one of the best known models is the approach
based on *Belief-Desire-Intention* (BDI) [15]. In the light of those efforts, multi-
agent programming has become a popular research topic in which researchers
aim at providing useful tools to express the behavior of agents. The Multi-Agent
Programming Contest (MAPC) has been created to evaluate and compare agent
systems [2].

For the 15th MAPC, which was held in 2020/2021, we improved the *Agents
Assemble* scenario [3] in order to make it challenging for former participants,
and as simple as possible for teams wanting to join the current contest. In total,
five teams participated in the 15th MAPC; three teams located in Europe, and

© Springer Nature Switzerland AG 2021
T. Ahlbrecht et al. (Eds.): MAPC 2021, LNAI 12947, pp. 3–20, 2021.
https://doi.org/10.1007/978-3-030-88549-6_1

two in South America. All teams but one chose specifically designed agent programming tools to develop their agents. Interestingly, that team was declared the winner of this edition.

1.1 Related Work and Competitions

Many competitions similar to the MAPC have been held, although in most of them the focus is not explicitly on multi-agent systems. We discuss some of the ones that are related to MAPC and still active.

Directly involving agents, the *(Power) Trading Agent Competition*[1] [13] provides a trading-related scenario in the energy market. However, each team only consists of a single "broker" agent, requiring no cooperation or coordination. The brokers compete with each other to attract more customers, in which they offer special tariffs for groups of customers. The goal here is to see how agents can autonomously solve supply-chain problems [14].

Probably the best-known are the various *RoboCup Simulation Leagues*[2]. RoboCup ranges over a variety of different domains like soccer, disaster response, assisting robots, and industrial logistics. Each league focuses on a specific problem that must be addressed by competitors. For instance, in RoboCupRescue two major leagues are organized on: (i) robots; and (ii) agent simulation. The first centers around (virtual) robots and less around abstract agents. For example, agents have noisy virtual sensors or may be subjected to complex physics, focusing on realism. The agent simulation league provides virtual agents placed on a map of a city that has been damaged by an earthquake event. Competitors focus on different self-isolated AI problems (e.g., task allocation) provided by the contest [17]. In addition, all teams have to give a presentation on their solution, which counts towards their final score.

We also mention a new challenge, the *Intention Progression Competition*[3] [7], which focuses on a specific issue within agent systems: the Intention Progression Problem, i.e. the decision of agents about how to proceed with their given intentions and plans in order to reach their goals. Thus, a solution for the MAPC (e.g. an agent) could be seen as a specific input challenge in the IPC, while solutions for the IPC could be used in agent platforms that participate in the MAPC.

When the focus comes to communication, we refer to the *Automated Negotiating Agent Competition*[4] [4]. In this competition, a participating team develops negotiation protocols and strategies and chose between a set of different flavors of competitions including agent-agent and human-agent negotiation. In this direction, HUMAINE[5] (Human Multi-Agent Immersive Negotiation Competition) focuses on multiple simultaneous negotiations between a human and competing agents [8].

---

[1] www.powertac.org.

[2] www.robocup.org.

[3] www.intentionprogression.org.

[4] http://ii.tudelft.nl/nego/node/7.

[5] https://cisl.rpi.edu/research/projects/humaine-human-multi-agent-immersive-negotiation.

There is also a number of challenges targeting specific problem domains. The *International Planning Competition* [16], has planning in the limelight, while in our contest it is only one possible component of an agent team. At the other end, the *General Game Playing* [9] competitions do not focus on one particular feature but on the ability of general AI systems to play an arbitrary game upon receiving its rules.

Finally, there are more than a few challenges focusing on finding (autonomous) solutions for existing commercial games, like the *Student StarCraft AI tournament*[6], or specifically designed games like *BattleCode*[7]. The goal here is usually to benchmark game AI techniques and algorithms. Not a competition but definitely worth mentioning is the *Blocks World for Teams* (BW4T) [12] environment, which has some relations to the current MAPC scenario. There, agents have to coordinate to deliver sequences of color-coded blocks.

1.2 Outline

This paper is organized as follows. Section 2 introduces the current setting for the Agents Assemble II scenario. In Sect. 3, we introduce how the 15th MAPC was organized. We present all participating teams as well as an overview on their performances. Section 4 aims at introducing some lessons we learned throughout the contest, regarding the overall organization and matches. Finally, in Sect. 5, we look at the future directions for the next MAPC.

2 The Current Setting

Our current scenario, titled *Agents Assemble II*, is an evolution of the previous one, played in the MAPC 2019 [3]. Each simulation is divided into a number of discrete steps. The primary elements of the game are agents and blocks situated in a two-dimensional grid environment. Each agent and each block inhabit exactly one cell of the grid. An agent can pick up a block from an adjacent cell and *attach* it to one of its four sides. The agent and the block then move together as one unit, whenever the agent moves. Two agents carrying blocks can connect these blocks if they are next to each other. Now one of the agents could disconnect from its block, leaving the other agent with two blocks to carry. Repeating this process a number of times, more complex two-dimensional shapes can be assembled out of blocks (see Fig. 1). Assembling specific shapes and delivering them to certain places on the grid is the main goal of both agent teams. The bigger the shape and the faster it is delivered, the more reward is paid out to the agent team. The simulation randomly generates tasks, i.e. the shapes that can be delivered at any point in time up to a deadline.

---

[6] www.sscaitournament.com.
[7] www.battlecode.org.

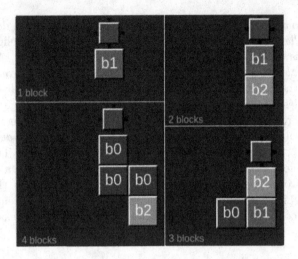

Fig. 1. Examples of different shapes and sizes required by tasks in the Agent Assemble scenario. The blue square represents an agent carrying all the blocks. (Color figure online)

2.1 Challenges

The central challenge of the scenario is how the agents can coordinate to complete a task. They need to determine which blocks to get and from where, how to assemble them into shapes with synchronized actions, and distribute these subtasks among themselves[8]. Blocks can be retrieved from *dispensers*, which are placed in randomized locations on the grid in each simulation. Similarly, the starting position of each agent and the shapes that need to be assembled are randomized.

Another challenging aspect of the scenario is each agent's perception or vision range. The agents only perceive things that are at most five blocks away, measured in Manhattan/taxicab distance. In addition, the agents do not perceive the team of other agents they encounter. Thus, if two agents meet, they need to ensure that they "know" each other. This is important for collaboration and also to merge their relative knowledge about the environment. All agents from one team can communicate freely (over any distance), though.

Each cell of the grid can also contain an *obstacle*, which prevents anything else from being at the same location. The obstacles are generated at the beginning of each simulation, forming a series of island-like structures on the grid. On the one hand, the obstacles complicate pathfinding, while on the other hand, they can serve as landmarks for agents to find their bearings. Additionally, agents may find themselves trapped if they are surrounded by obstacles. In such a

---

[8] The complete scenario description with all action and percept descriptions can be found at https://github.com/agentcontest/massim_2020/blob/master/docs/scenario.md.

case, they would have to use the *clear* action to remove single obstacles. In a similar fashion, *clear events* randomly occur in the environment. They remove all obstacles in a certain area and scatter new obstacles around, dynamically changing the environment. This makes it harder for agents to know for certain if they are in a position where another agent of their team had already been before.

Finally, not to be underestimated, the presence of another agent team can have a huge impact, as those agents are usually highly unpredictable. In the basic case, the two teams at least compete for the same tasks. Any task that is completed immediately becomes unavailable for the other team as well. But the other agents might implement a strategy that aims to disturb their opponents. For example, they could try to hit them with *clear* actions, which would disable them for a couple of steps. More generally, the goal zones are likely points of contention. If an agent can be kept out of the goal zone, it cannot deliver its task in time.

2.2 Modifications

As we use the Agent Assemble scenario for the second time in a row, we considered the following in order to modify the previous setting for the new edition:

1. how can we improve the scenario, possibly mitigating major advantages of winning strategies; and
2. how do we keep the scenario as simple as possible so that we make it easier for new teams to participate.

Given that, we designed and implemented some modifications and, as usual, iterated over it a few times to reach a mature and stable setting. The changes were as follows:

- The grid's bounds were removed. Now, if an agent were to move off the grid, it would just appear on the opposite side, making it harder for the agents to find out their absolute positions.
- *Task boards* where introduced, were agents have to go to accept a task. Each agent can only accept one task at a time and an agent can only submit a task that it has accepted itself. We made this change to keep agents from staying in a *goal zone* (where tasks are to be delivered) all the time: a behavior that could often be seen in the previous Contest. It may also give some insight into the agent's intentions.
- Previously, the reward of a task only depended on its size. To be precise, let t^{req} be the number of blocks a task t requires, then its reward r^t is given by $r^t = 10 \times (t^{req})^2$. Now, to give to faster agents an advantage, the reward of each task decreases in each step according to a decay rate. For instance, if the reward decay rate is set to 50% and the current reward for a given task t is $r^t = 10$, in the next step, it decreases to $r^t = 5$. This process continues for any given task t until some predefined percentage of its original reward is reached; for instance, 10% of the original value.

- To speed up the start of the game, agents are now very likely to start close to one or more agents from their team. Doing so, they might immediately start working in smaller groups.
- To ensure fairness in the beginning of a simulation, agents of different teams share the same cell on the grid. That is, let m be the number of teams, then any cell that is a starting location for an agent will contain exactly m agents; one agent of each team. This is only allowed in the beginning of a simulation as in the remaining steps no agent can share a cell with any other agent; regardless if they are teammates.

3   The Tournament

The actual Contest, originally planned for the end of the year 2020, had to be delayed due to various reasons; the main one probably is the pandemic. Thus, the 15th MAPC (formerly titled MAPC 2020) took place on the 15th and 16th March 2021.

3.1   Overall Organization

As always, the contest is organized into 3 phases: (1) registration; (2) qualification; and (3) the contest itself. The registration aims at introducing the teams one to the other, in which each team briefly describes itself to the general public pointing out the technologies they intend to use.

In the qualification phase, a team of agents play two subsequent simulations alone in the contest scenario. The team must submit at least one task in each of the two simulations and send most of their actions in time (i.e., 70% of all actions must arrive at the contest server in which the deadline per action is set up at 4 s). Both simulations last for 300 steps, and the tasks require 2 or 3 blocks to be assembled together. In the first simulation, the team coordinates 15 agents, and in the second 50 agents.

Finally, in the contest each team plays one match against each other participating team. One match consists of three simulations with different parameters. The simulations mainly differ in the number of agents and the size of the grid. In the first simulation of each match, every team has 15 agents, in the second 30 and in the final simulation 50 agents at their disposal. During a match, both teams are allowed to monitor only action results (e.g., action completed successfully). That means the teams cannot observe the grid itself, and hence, what the opponent agents are doing. Also, they may reconnect their agents in any case of bugs and connection failures, although the simulation never stops increasing steps after a deadline (4 s). After the contest is finished, all teams come together to watch how they performed during the matches.

Ultimately, five teams were able to pass the qualification and participate in the Contest.

3.2 Participants

We give a brief overview of each team and their agent solution in alphabetical order.

FIT BUT. The team from Brno University of Technology from Czech Republic consists of three members. They already participated in the MAPC 2019 and built on their earlier team, which is written entirely in Java. This makes them the only team, this time, that did not use a dedicated agent programming language or platform. Their solution is comparable to BDI agents, though. They invested approximately 130 h to upgrade their previous solution to the new scenario, producing 7461 lines of code, up almost 2000 lines from 2019.

GOAL-DTU. The team from the Technical University of Denmark, one of the most regular MAPC contenders, consists of five members, two of which made up the 2019 *GOAL-DTU* team. As their name suggests, they made use of the well-known GOAL agent programming language [10]. GOAL is based on the notions of beliefs and goals and supports rule-based decision making. The team's code base roughly doubled in size, to a still compact 2000 lines. About 460 h were spent updating and improving their agents, a lot of which fell to updating to a new version of GOAL.

JaCaMo Builders. The team from Federal University of Santa Catarina, Santa Catarina State University and Federal Institute of Santa Catarina, Brazil, and Umeå University, Sweden, consists of nine members, who were new to the scenario, however, many of which already participated in earlier editions of the Contest. Their agents were created with the JaCaMo agent platform [6]. JaCaMo combines multiple agent techniques in a single framework. The prevalent agent platform Jason is used for programming the agents. CArtAgO is included to deal with environments, while Moise handles the organizational level. The team invested about 1000 h into creating their agent team. This is the most time spent of any team in this MAPC, but as this team also has the most members, and didn't have a previous solution to build on, it is not surprising. The size of their code, 5914 lines of Jason, 947 lines for CArtAgO and another 1258 lines of Java code, is comparable to the solution of *FIT BUT* and about four times that of *GOAL-DTU*.

LTI-USP. The team from University of São Paulo, Brazil, is the smallest team with only two members. They spent about 400 h developing 1985 lines of Jason code, a solution as compact as the one of *GOAL-DTU*. *LTI-USP* was the other newcomer besides *JaCaMo Builders*, creating their agent team entirely from scratch.

MLFC. The team from University of Manchester and University of Liverpool, UK, University of Genova, Italy, Lancaster University Leipzig, Germany, and Maynooth University, Ireland, consists of six members, three of which already participated in the previous Contest (one among them who also participated a couple of times even before). They built on their previous JaCaMo entry, resulting in approximately 3000 more lines of code and 9805 in total, even more than that of *JaCaMo Builders*. Their Java part grew more than the

Jason part, though. They invested around 200 h this time.

An important part of their system is still the Fast-Downward planner, which they use to plan long distance movement.

All teams this time more or less programmed some sort of BDI agents. They either directly used a BDI agent platform or adopted a BDI-like programming style. In addition, we only saw approaches that took a more or less decentralized perspective, the difference being that some agents subscribe to a (dynamic) group and follow their chosen group leader's orders, while other agents make up their own goals and ask for help, e.g. via auctions.

3.3   Final Ranking

Each simulation awarded three points to the winner (the team that earns the highest sum of task rewards), or one point to both teams in case of a draw. With each team playing four matches of three simulations each, this makes a maximum achievable score of 36 points.

After taking home the second place in 2019, *FIT BUT* achieved first place in the 15th MAPC with a clear lead of 30 points. The second place is shared by *GOAL-DTU* and *MLFC*, who were both able to score 22 points. The third place went to *LTI-USP* with 9 points and fourth place to *JaCaMo Builders* with 6 points. The results are again summarized in Table 1.

Table 1. The ranking of the 15th MAPC

Place	Team	Points	Wins	Draws	FIT BUT	GOAL-DTU	MLFC	LTI-USP	JaCaMo Builders
1	FIT BUT	30	10	—	—	6:3	6:3	9:0	9:0
2	GOAL-DTU	22	7	1	3:6	—	7:1	6:3	6:3
	MLFC	22	7	1	3:6	1:7	—	9:0	9:0
3	LTI-USP	9	3	—	0:9	3:6	0:9	—	6:3
4	JaCaMo Builders	6	2	—	0:9	3:6	0:9	3:6	—

We note that no team was completely undefeated and no team ended up without any victory.

3.4   Team Performance

Given the results above, we analyze how the teams reached their scores. To do so, we consider the tasks submitted by each team during a match alongside the number of noActions, which might indicate bugs on the team's side or poor connection. A noAction means that an agent failed to submit an action in time for the current step. The numbers are given in detail in Table 2.

Table 2. Performance of the participating teams in each match. The columns R1, R2, R3, and R4 mean the number of submitted tasks containing 1, 2, 3, and 4 requirements respectively.

FIT BUT vs. *JaCaMo Builders*

	Score	R1	R2	R3	R4	noActions
Sim. 1	38 : 0	6 : 0	1 : 0	1 : 0	0 : 0	1770 : 375
Sim. 2	113 : 8	4 : 0	1 : 1	3 : 0	1 : 0	2100 : 836
Sim. 3	98 : 0	15 : 0	4 : 0	2 : 0	0 : 0	5642 : 4364

GOAL-DTU vs. *LTI-USP*

	Score	R1	R2	R3	R4	noActions
Sim. 1	65 : 16	0 : 4	3 : 1	1 : 0	0 : 0	0 : 7
Sim. 2	100 : 14	0 : 3	6 : 1	1 : 0	0 : 0	30 : 493
Sim. 3	0 : 38	0 : 3	0 : 4	0 : 0	0 : 0	105 : 689

FIT BUT vs. *MLFC*

	Score	R1	R2	R3	R4	noActions
Sim. 1	0 : 48	0 : 1	0 : 1	0 : 2	0 : 0	306 : 75
Sim. 2	53 : 44	9 : 0	4 : 1	0 : 2	0 : 0	465 : 5450
Sim. 3	90 : 18	11 : 0	4 : 0	2 : 1	0 : 0	1676 : 8684

JaCaMo Builders vs. *LTI-USP*

	Score	R1	R2	R3	R4	noActions
Sim. 1	8 : 0	4 : 0	0 : 0	0 : 0	0 : 0	57 : 125
Sim. 2	10 : 20	5 : 2	0 : 2	0 : 0	0 : 0	576 : 298
Sim. 3	10 : 18	5 : 1	0 : 2	0 : 0	0 : 0	1480 : 264

GOAL-DTU vs. *MLFC*

	Score	R1	R2	R3	R4	noActions
Sim. 1	187 : 26	0 : 0	6 : 1	3 : 1	1 : 0	15 : 41
Sim. 2	0 : 0	0 : 0	0 : 0	0 : 0	0 : 0	88 : 3889
Sim. 3	105 : 48	0 : 0	2 : 0	4 : 1	0 : 0	363 : 12314

FIT BUT vs. *GOAL-DTU*

	Score	R1	R2	R3	R4	noActions
Sim. 1	62 : 181	7 : 0	2 : 4	0 : 1	1 : 2	124 : 11
Sim. 2	104 : 0	8 : 0	7 : 0	1 : 0	0 : 0	437 : 30
Sim. 3	282 : 0	13 : 0	13 : 0	4 : 0	1 : 0	780 : 209

GOAL-DTU vs. *JaCaMo Builders*

	Score	R1	R2	R3	R4	noActions
Sim. 1	353 : 10	0 : 5	8 : 0	4 : 0	4 : 0	0 : 80
Sim. 2	235 : 12	0 : 6	5 : 0	4 : 0	2 : 0	35 : 107
Sim. 3	0 : 8	0 : 4	0 : 0	0 : 0	0 : 0	398 : 1951

FIT BUT vs. *LTI-USP*

	Score	R1	R2	R3	R4	noActions
Sim. 1	185 : 16	9 : 0	1 : 2	7 : 0	0 : 0	136 : 6
Sim. 2	148 : 10	10 : 1	8 : 1	0 : 0	2 : 0	487 : 123
Sim. 3	314 : 0	7 : 0	13 : 0	4 : 0	3 : 0	3242 : 636

JaCaMo Builders vs. *MLFC*

	Score	R1	R2	R3	R4	noActions
Sim. 1	10 : 60	5 : 1	0 : 1	0 : 1	0 : 1	69 : 82
Sim. 2	10 : 26	5 : 0	0 : 1	0 : 1	0 : 0	745 : 1499
Sim. 3	10 : 148	5 : 0	0 : 3	0 : 3	0 : 1	1376 : 5684

LTI-USP vs. *MLFC*

	Score	R1	R2	R3	R4	noActions
Sim. 1	12 : 160	2 : 1	1 : 0	0 : 4	0 : 1	102 : 60
Sim. 2	38 : 195	7 : 2	3 : 5	0 : 2	0 : 2	283 : 2650
Sim. 3	8 : 235	0 : 0	1 : 2	0 : 3	0 : 3	734 : 5529

We see that the number of missing actions generally increases with the number of agents the teams had at their disposal (15, 30 and 50 per simulation).

By total counts, we see *MLFC* in the lead, as they had to battle with connection problems a number of times. *FIT BUT* follows and then *JaCaMo Builders*. *LTI-USP* and *GOAL-DTU* had rather few noActions, while *GOAL-DTU* even managed to play two entire simulations without any action missing.

FIT BUT usually showed the sharpest rise in noActions from the second to the third simulation. Though, the only simulations they lost were the first ones against *GOAL-DTU* and *MLFC*, where they only had a moderate amount of noActions.

GOAL-DTU on the other hand saw also saw their biggest percentage increase from the second to the third simulation and these were also the simulations that *GOAL-DTU* lost against both *JaCaMo Builders* and *LTI-USP*, suggesting a bigger disadvantage with 50 agents for *GOAL-DTU*.

In the direct comparison of *JaCaMo Builders* and *LTI-USP*, we see that the *JaCaMo Builders* won the first simulation where they usually had a very low count of noActions. While they increased in the next simulations, *LTI-USP* had a less severe rise in the second simulation and even a decrease again in the third.

While the number of noActions may indicate problems the teams had with certain team sizes, we are happy to see that this was for many matches, maybe all, only one of many factors deciding how the match concluded.

Regarding the submission of tasks, we see, in general, the number of submitted tasks is proportional to their complexity. That means, tasks of lower complexity are more likely to be submitted by the teams. *JaCaMo Builders* and *LTI-USP* took it one step further and use it as their underlying strategy. They worked only on tasks of low complexity (namely containing 1 or 2 requirements), which did not pay off in the end (see Table 1). However, it was sufficient to reach victories when the opponent team was in difficulties. For instance, in the third simulation of the match *GOAL-DTU* versus *JaCaMo Builders*, the latter won the simulation by submitting 4 single-block tasks while *GOAL-DTU* did not submit anything. Moreover, when it comes to the first simulation, we can see that no team was a match for *GOAL-DTU*, as they won all of their first simulations.

3.5 Selected Matches

Given the overall results introduced above, we discuss how the teams approached the challenging problem of this edition of the MAPC. Our overview provides only a viewpoint from outsiders. For more details about all matches, we refer the reader to the description paper of each participating team.

MLFC vs. FIT BUT. In this match, *MLFC* took the first simulation from the champion-to-be *FIT BUT*, for a score of 3:6. After a short exploration phase, both teams preemptively started picking up blocks. *FIT BUT* was the first to have an agent accepting a task, in step 111/750. 50 steps later, that agent met another agent in order to complete the desired pattern. However, with the deadline approaching, at step 182, they could not find and reach a goal zone in time. Shortly after, two *FIT BUT* agents appeared to be stuck in a navigation conflict that would persist throughout the simulation (see Fig. 2). The remaining agents still tried to pursue other goals.

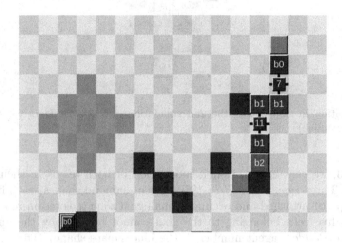

Fig. 2. Heavily packed *FIT BUT* agents are stuck between unusually close task boards.

In the meantime, *MLFC* had selected one goal zone to defend and another to submit tasks. After accepting a task, one agent waited for deliveries in the dedicated goal zone, while agents holding blocks waited in a formation next to the goal. The first task was accepted in step 227 and completed in step 260.

In the two following simulations, *FIT BUT* agents were able to carry out their strategy much more effectively. In general, they aggressively accepted more concurrent tasks and completed them more quickly. *MLFC* on the other hand was the most robust team in this contest, considering the number of simulations with at least one completed task, but could not quite keep pace with *FIT BUT*.

***JaCaMo Builders* vs. *LTI-USP*.** This match-up went 6:3 to *LTI-USP*. *JaCaMo Builders* showed very consistent performance over all three simulations, completing four to five tasks in every simulation, each one with a size of 1 and reward 2. *LTI-USP* wasn't able to complete any tasks in the first simulation. In the second and third games, *LTI-USP* completed fewer tasks (4 and 3) than *JaCaMo Builders* (5 each), but in both simulations, two of the tasks were of size 2 and reward 8, yielding the decisive lead. The *JaCaMo Builders* showed different behavior in the second simulation, attaching multiple blocks at once to the same agent. Overall though, the *LTI-USP* agents seemed to be carrying more blocks around. Interestingly, in the third simulation, *LTI-USP* completed their third and final task in step 245, while *JaCaMo Builders* completed their first task more than 300 steps later, in step 568 (and followed with four more tasks).

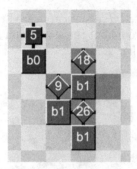

Fig. 3. Situation in step 510 of the 2nd simulation *JaCaMo Builders* vs. *LTI-USP* (Color figure online)

In Fig. 3, we can see an implicit interaction of both teams in their second simulation. Three agents from *LTI-USP* (green diamond shapes) each have one block of type b1 attached and occupy a small goal zone (colored in red) so that four of the five cells belonging to the goal cannot be used by the approaching *JaCaMo Builders* agent number 5 (the blue square shape). This agent has accepted task 22, which requires a single b0 block to be delivered. The *LTI-USP* agents continue working in the goal zone almost until the task's deadline in step 595, making it nearly impossible for their opponent to complete its task. The *JaCaMo Builders* agent also stops sending any actions. Only after the deadline has passed, it gives up on its block and task and moves on.

FIT BUT vs. GOAL-DTU. This match opened up the second day of matches for the MAPC. At that time *FIT BUT* was leading the contest (15 points) followed closely by *GOAL-DTU* (13 points). Therefore, the outcome of this match could seal off the fate of the 15th MAPC.

In the first simulation, *FIT BUT* scored first and seemed to be dominating the game. For instance, at step 121 (see Fig. 4), agent *GOAL-DTU_13* had finished assembling a set of blocks in the required shape to submit a task and hence earn a reward of 19 for it. However, agent *FIT BUT_1* managed to clear all blocks from *GOAL-DTU_13* right before the submission take place, which resulted in a failed action for *GOAL-DTU_13*. However, it turned out that *FIT BUT* could not keep the pace with clearing the opponent's blocks at the goal zone. As a result, *GOAL-DTU* won the first simulation by scoring 181 against 62 from *FIT BUT*.

Quite interestingly, *GOAL-DTU* had problems during the second and third simulations to submit tasks; in fact, they submitted none. However, that was not a problem for *FIT BUT* who was declared the winner with a large lead: 104:0 in the second simulation and 282:0 in the third simulation. Although we notice an increase in missed actions from *GOAL-DTU* in the two last simulations (11 actions in the first, 30 in the second, and 209 actions in the third), connection issues were not the main reason for *GOAL-DTU*'s behavior.

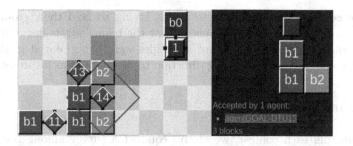

Fig. 4. First simulation of the match between *FIT BUT* vs. *GOAL-DTU*. *GOAL-DTU*'s agents (numbers 13, 14, and 11, in green), at the goal zone in red, are assembling the required 'L' shape for a task submission while a *FIT BUT* agent (number 1, in blue) performs a `clear` action on them at step 122. (Color figure online)

According to them [11], during those simulations they encountered serious bugs, which they were not able to manage in the remaining of that match.

3.6 Free-for-All

After the contest we invited all teams to participate in two experimental simulations, where all teams would play at the same time in the same environment. Four out of the five teams showed up for the games. The parameters were comparable to those of the tournament simulations, only with slightly bigger maps (from 70 × 70 cells to 80 × 80 in the first, and from 80 × 80 to 90 × 90 in the second) to account for much more agents. Two simulations were run with 15 and 30 agents per team.

In the first simulation, *FIT BUT* completed some tasks early on, but was soon overtaken by *GOAL-DTU*, who were able to submit two tasks of size 4 consecutively. During the following phase of around 250 steps, *GOAL-DTU* completed four tasks and *JaCaMo Builders* one, while *FIT BUT* did not submit anything. In the remaining 250 steps, *FIT BUT* completed another nine jobs (unlike everyone else), but the tasks were only of sizes one or two, which in the end did not suffice to pull ahead of *GOAL-DTU*.

It appears that *FIT BUT*'s aggressively working on small tasks made it also very difficult for *JaCaMo Builders*. In the second simulation, *FIT BUT* showed more consistent performance, leaving less opportunities for the other teams. They completed 25 tasks, while *GOAL-DTU* submitted three and *JaCaMo Builders* two. Unfortunately, the *MLFC* agents were not able to score. In the first simulation, one group of their agents was interrupted by *GOAL-DTU* clear actions (returning the favor to *GOAL-DTU* afterwards). In the second simulation, they showed rather defensive behavior around some of the goal zones.

Asking the teams about their experiences, they note that disruptive strategies are probably not so efficient anymore, as they cannot interfere with all other teams at the same time. Also, more (adversarial) agents in the same environment raises new issues. Specific to the current scenario, the goal zones have become even more contested areas with four teams trying to hold their ground. The overall takeaway from our experiment is that the teams' strategies were not as effective, now that multiple different strategies were being played in the same grid. This points out an interesting direction to be adopted in future contests.

4   Lessons Learned

After organizing each contest, we always conduct a survey among the participants to collect information about all aspects of the contest. In particular about: the team itself, the effort needed to get the team of agents running, technologies and strategies, and finally, general questions about the contest. The reader will find the teams' responses to the questionnaire in the corresponding team description paper.

All teams pointed out that the MAPC is an opportunity to learn more about agent programming, get some hands-on experience or even evaluate their own scientific work related to agent programming.

As the 15th MAPC is the second version of the Agents Assemble scenario, we discuss in the following how our modifications to the previous setting affected the new contest. Then, we discuss the overall lessons learned from the current setting.

4.1   A New Version of the Agents Assemble Scenario

Given the modifications introduced in Sect. 2.2, we discuss how they have affected the teams' plays and therefore the matches.

An endless grid proved to be challenging for all teams, regardless whether they participated in the previous edition or not. In the survey responses, those teams, namely *GOAL-DTU*, *FIT BUT* and *MLFC*, stated they had to adapt their exploration strategies accordingly. A task board addressed a naive strategy of keeping an agent always in the goal zone for submitting tasks. While forcing agents to explicitly commit to a task with the `accept` action, it remains unclear which agents are actually cooperating in any given moment to submit a particular task.

Regarding the reward decreasing, it aimed at posing decision making challenges to the agents. However, after asking the teams directly about this feature, whether they have considered it or not, we found out that most of them ignored it and worked on new incoming tasks only. *GOAL-DTU* takes it into account while deciding which task to accept (based on an estimation of steps needed to accomplish it), and once accepted, they intend to submit it unless the deadline is reached. On the other hand, *FIT BUT* always evaluates the tasks' current rewards at every step, which leads them to consider the reward decay feature indirectly.

4.2 The 15th MAPC

Regarding the MAPC as a whole, from an observer perspective, understanding the joint behavior of the agents is still challenging. Even though we have implemented this year an agent view in which only a selected agent is in focus in the monitor, it is not enough to fully understand what is going on. While in the newest game (i.e., agents assemble scenario), it is easier than in other scenarios to see what actually happens (e.g. in the earlier *City scenario* [1]), the increase in the number of agents this time made it much more difficult, again, to get a clear picture of the agents' cooperation and coordination. Therefore, it is not only the characteristics of a given scenario that poses difficulties for understanding the joint approach of the agents.

In the same direction, we noted that *debugging* agent systems is still considered by many teams one of the most time consuming and difficult task. This has been the case in all contests since the very beginning [2]. The lack of sophisticated tools often leaves no other choice than to use logging statements to understand what went wrong. Debugging is particularly important in this edition because, for the second contest in a row, we prevented the team members from observing the environment during the matches. Instead, they get insights only from the information their agents receive. In case a team needs more than logging statements, they are left to implement some sort of custom monitor to keep up with the agents' status. Debugging is even harder if multiple languages and tools are combined, as mentioned by *MLFC*. Fortunately, Jason added recently a new feature to address such a problem: assertions, which is mentioned by *JaCaMo Builders*.

Moreover, if the teams had more time, most would have spend it on fixing bugs first instead of developing new features. Testing a multi-agent system is very challenging, and thus, new or previously undiscovered issues can arise at any point. The Contest is usually a new situation for all participating agents, as they cannot have been possibly tested in the same environment with the other agent team(s).

5 Outlook

In Sect. 4, we noticed that coordination and cooperation are still difficult tasks to monitor during the matches. The characteristics of a scenario affect them directly. For instance, in the cow herding scenario it is easy to realize which agents are cooperating as they push the cows towards a corral [5]. On the other hand, in the agents assemble scenario, it is not easy to determine which agents cooperate at all (from a simple observer perspective). In the end, one can safely assume teamwork if the agents managed to successfully cooperate on a task, but if they failed in between, there is barely no outside indication of that attempt. In future work we aim at addressing this issue.

It has been for a long time a desire to organize a contest in which many teams play at the same time and in the same environment. In Sect. 3.6, we described our experiment towards this goal. While we did not plan this in a very detailed way, rather we decided ad hoc to do it, we believe it has been a success. Therefore, matches containing many teams playing together is a feasible direction that we are strongly considering. For one, we could see all teams playing at once under similar circumstances, which could save considerable time, both in running the competition and analyzing it. Then again, the scenario needs to be very carefully designed to account for more than two direct competitors: this cannot be just an afterthought. Imagine two teams "battling" each other while a third team manages to play the game mostly undisturbed in a separate location. In this case, the success of the third team could be more ascribed to chance, and so, a very good scenario would need to prevent such things. As we can see, the current scenario would need considerable changes. Additionally, it would be even more interesting to see dynamic coalitions among agents from many different teams. As of now, we are not sure how to build such a mechanism into a scenario, that would still be competitive and fair to all parties.

For its very first edition, the participants of the MAPC had to submit their agent code, which was run by the organizers. This had the benefit that all agents were running on the same hardware and there was no additional delay due to networking. Unfortunately, this proved to be quite difficult and time-consuming, as the organizers had to know exactly how to run each agent team. Now however, with containerization and new methods of virtualization being a hot topic, it appears reasonable to think about this approach again. The teams could submit their agents in some kind of container or prepare them inside a virtual machine directly on the contest server. For one, this would be the only way to ensure that agents are running in almost the same conditions in terms of hardware and network. History has shown that the delay can be quite extensive for some teams.

We might need to adapt the scenario to be a bit more forgiving, since the agent operators would not be able to intervene during a simulation (mostly by restarting the agents if they get stuck due to a previously undetected bug or just an unforeseen situation). This is also a new challenge in terms of autonomy, that has not been required as much so far. It would certainly be interesting to see how the participants deal with this, how they improve stability and robustness and which methods of repair and recovery they come up with.

Additionally, we are quite limited in what kinds of simulations we can run using the current approach, as the presence of the organizers and competing teams is required during the whole match. If this could be automated, we could have the agents play many more and also much longer games. At the same time, we would then need better (i.e. more automated) means of analysis, as there would be many more simulations to analyze.

Acknowledgment. The authors would like to thank Alfred Hofmann from Springer for his continuous support right from the beginning, and for endowing the prize of 500 Euros in Springer books.

Also, we extend our gratitude to all anonymous reviewers who helped us make improvements to this paper.

The fourth author acknowledges that his part in this study was financed by the Coordenação de Aperfeiçoamento de Pessoal de Nível Superior - Brasil (CAPES) - Finance Code 001.

References

1. Ahlbrecht, T., Dix, J., Fiekas, N.: Multi-agent programming contest 2016. Int. J. Agent-Oriented Softw. Eng. **6**(1), 58–85 (2018)
2. Ahlbrecht, T., Dix, J., Fiekas, N., Krausburg, T.: Accept a challenge: the multi-agent programming contest. In: Baroglio, C., Hubner, J.F., Winikoff, M. (eds.) EMAS 2020. LNCS (LNAI), vol. 12589, pp. 129–143. Springer, Cham (2020). https://doi.org/10.1007/978-3-030-66534-0_9
3. Ahlbrecht, T., Dix, J., Fiekas, N., Krausburg, T. (eds.): The Multi-Agent Programming Contest 2019: Agents Assemble - Block by Block to Victory, 1st edn. Springer, Cham (2020). https://doi.org/10.1007/978-3-030-59299-8
4. Aydoğan, R., et al.: Challenges and main results of the automated negotiating agents competition (ANAC) 2019. In: Bassiliades, N., Chalkiadakis, G., de Jonge, D. (eds.) EUMAS/AT-2020. LNCS (LNAI), vol. 12520, pp. 366–381. Springer, Cham (2020). https://doi.org/10.1007/978-3-030-66412-1_23
5. Behrens, T., Dastani, M., Dix, J., Köster, M., Novák, P.: The multi-agent programming contest from 2005–2010. Ann. Math. Artif. Intell. **59**(3–4), 277–311 (2010). https://doi.org/10.1007/s10472-010-9219-5
6. Boissier, O., Bordini, R.H., Hübner, J.F., Ricci, A., Santi, A.: Multi-agent oriented programming with JaCaMo. Sci. Comput. Program. **78**(6), 747–761 (2013)
7. Castle-Green, S., Dewfall, A., Logan, B.: The intention progression competition. In: Baroglio, C., Hubner, J.F., Winikoff, M. (eds.) EMAS 2020. LNCS (LNAI), vol. 12589, pp. 144–151. Springer, Cham (2020). https://doi.org/10.1007/978-3-030-66534-0_10
8. Divekar, R.R., et al.: HUMAINE: human multi-agent immersive negotiation competition. In: Extended Abstracts of the 2020 CHI Conference on Human Factors in Computing Systems, CHI EA 2020, pp. 1–10. Association for Computing Machinery, New York (2020). https://doi.org/10.1145/3334480.3383001
9. Genesereth, M., Love, N., Pell, B.: General game playing: overview of the AAAI competition. AI Mag. **26**(2), 62 (2005)
10. Hindriks, K.V.: Programming rational agents in GOAL. In: El Fallah Seghrouchni, A., Dix, J., Dastani, M., Bordini, R.H. (eds.) Multi-Agent Programming, pp. 119–157. Springer, Boston, MA (2009). https://doi.org/10.1007/978-0-387-89299-3_4
11. Jensen, A.B., Villadsen, J., Weile, J., Gylling, E.K.: The 15th edition of the multi-agent programming contest - the GOAL-DTU team (2021)
12. Johnson, M., Jonker, C., van Riemsdijk, B., Feltovich, P.J., Bradshaw, J.M.: Joint activity testbed: blocks world for teams (BW4T). In: Aldewereld, H., Dignum, V., Picard, G. (eds.) ESAW 2009. LNCS (LNAI), vol. 5881, pp. 254–256. Springer, Heidelberg (2009). https://doi.org/10.1007/978-3-642-10203-5_26
13. Ketter, W., Collins, J., Reddy, P.: Power TAC: a competitive economic simulation of the smart grid. Energy Econ. **39**, 262–270 (2013)
14. Ketter, W., Collins, J., de Weerdt, M.: The 2020 power trading agent competition. ERIM Rep. Ser. Ref., (2020-002), 0–47 (2020)

15. Rao, A.S., Georgeff, M.P., et al.: BDI agents: from theory to practice. In: ICMAS, vol. 95, pp. 312–319 (1995)
16. Vallati, M., Chrpa, L., Grześ, M., McCluskey, T.L., Roberts, M., Sanner, S., et al.: The 2014 international planning competition: progress and trends. AI Mag. **36**(3), 90–98 (2015)
17. Visser, A., Ito, N., Kleiner, A.: RoboCup rescue simulation innovation strategy. In: Bianchi, R.A.C., Akin, H.L., Ramamoorthy, S., Sugiura, K. (eds.) RoboCup 2014. LNCS (LNAI), vol. 8992, pp. 661–672. Springer, Cham (2015). https://doi.org/10.1007/978-3-319-18615-3_54

Participants

FIT BUT: Rational Agents in the Multi-Agent Programming Contest

Vaclav Uhlir[✉][iD], Frantisek Zboril[iD], and Frantisek Vidensky[iD]

Department of Intelligent Systems, Faculty of Information Technology,
Brno University of Technology, Brno, Czech Republic
{iuhlir,zborilf,ividensky}@fit.vutbr.cz
https://www.fit.vut.cz/.en

Abstract. The 2020 Multi-Agent Programming Contest introduced a modified scenario from last year - Agents Assemble II. Teams of agents compete against each other in completing tasks that consists of assembling blocks into desired structures. In this paper, we describe our strategy, system design, and improvements we made over last year. This paper also contains a description of the tournament matches from our point of view.

Keywords: Artificial Intelligence · Multi-Agent Programming · Decision-making Planning · Self-organisation · Rational Agents

1 Introduction

The Multi-Agent Programming Contest (MAPC)[1], which has been organized since 2005, aims to stimulate research in the area of multi-agent systems. The contest is divided into phases for which it releases new scenarios. These scenarios are released for each phase, modified every year, and specify the entire contest.

Contestants must identify key problems and create a multi-agent system to score as many points as possible. In each match, two teams compete against each other in three rounds/simulations. Teams can build their systems on any framework/programming language they want. These systems communicate with the server using JSON messages. Each simulation has a certain number of steps. For each step, agents can send the required action to the server within a certain time interval. At the beginning of the next step, they receive the result of the action and new percepts.

The scenario for this year was named "Agents Assemble II". In this scenario, agents must face limited local vision and ignorance of the global position (they only perceive objects at a certain distance to their relative position). The environment is a rectangular grid which loops horizontally and vertically. Thus, if an agent moves off the right edge of the map, it will appear on the left side and this situation is not detectable by the agent. The environment is dynamic - during

---

[1] https://multiagentcontest.org/.

© Springer Nature Switzerland AG 2021
T. Ahlbrecht et al. (Eds.): MAPC 2021, LNAI 12947, pp. 23–45, 2021.
https://doi.org/10.1007/978-3-030-88549-6_2

the course of the simulation, events can occur that destroy or create obstacles and can disable agents and/or strip them of their cargo.

Agents must complete certain tasks to score points. Tasks appear randomly during the simulation. Each agent can hold only one accepted task, and only an agent holding a specific task can submit it. Each task defines a complex structure made of blocks that must be assembled and delivered to a goal area. An agent can retrieve a block of a certain kind from a dispenser of said kind. Agents must cooperate to be able to assemble nontrivial structures and additional synchronization and cooperation is critical for agents effectiveness. The implementation of effective cooperation is the core of the contest.

Our team has already gained experience from last year's contest, where we achieved second place. We created two systems [5]. The first of the systems was a proactive system that worked with pre-specified scenarios and tasks agents with generated goals designed for individual agents according to assigned role. The second system was designed as more reactive and employed layered architecture with highly dynamic behaviour, where agents chose their action based on their perception of the usefulness of said action. This architecture is similar to Subsumption architecture [1], but it also deals with the symbolic representation of environments and plans.

We chose the second system as more suitable for the contest. This year, we fixed some bugs we discovered during last year's competition. And we have improved and adapted the system for this year's scenario. With these modifications and improvements of the system, we were able to achieve first place in this year's competition.

This paper is organised in sections focused on the parts of system design – more specifically: strategy 2.1, agent synchronization 2.2, map construction 2.3, agent reasoning cycle 2.4, goals and plans 2.5 and the action reservation system 2.6. This will be followed by an analysis of the matches, a discussion of the limits and possible improvements to the system.

2   System Design

This section describes the key ideas on which our system was built. As mentioned above, we decided to improve our system that we developed for last year's competition. The basic idea on which our system is based is described in the last year's article [5], but this paper will summarize all important parts for the sake of coherent system description.

As some members of our research group focus on BDI [4] agent systems, we considered whether to build our solution on top of an existing BDI solution. In the end, we decided to create our own system. The environment of last year's and this year's scenario is highly dynamic. We realized that implementing a complex agent with specific roles and long term plans might not be the right choice in such environment. And a simpler more reactive agent would be more appropriate for this type of scenario.

For the implementation of the system, we chose the Java language and used *BasicAgent* template to create our own agent system platform. There were several reasons for choosing this. Most of the team members already had experience with Java language. It has a good ratio between performance and development time and it is also easy to synchronize threads in Java. Each agent and other elements of the system runs in its thread, so it would be possible to expand the system to run on multiple machines, but as our system performed good enough on single machine, this option remains on possible future enhancements if needed.

2.1 Strategies

Our system is based on a relatively simple strategy of use of multitasking to achieve as many goals as possible at once. While exploring the environment, agents may find dispensers or blocks of various types. At the same time, the most complex (and time-consuming) task would be to acquire blocks only when an agent has an active task. In this case, it would be necessary to plan exactly which agent gets which block. And given the dynamics of the environment, where the terrain could change at any moment and an agent would have to find another way, it would be difficult to synchronize all the agents so that the necessary blocks are safely collected as soon as possible.

We have decided to merge these processes. We base our system on the assumption that the vast majority of tasks can be completed only using blocks that agents collect while exploring the environment. More complex tasks are less likely to be completed this way. However, if our agents are able to complete a large number of simple tasks in a short time, they would earn more points than by completing complex tasks at length – fast completing of simpler task also lowers the chance of enemy intercepting our agents or submitting the task faster.

This is achieved by agents gradually attaching blocks of different types to their bodies – these block can be either picked up from the environment or requested from dispensers. When an agent accepts a task, other near agents with required missing blocks are contacted and agents create plans for the fastest meeting point to hand off and attach blocks.

As described in the introduction, agents do not know their global position and only know the position of other near objects relative to their position in the environment. In this state, no multi-agent planning, even this simplistic, is possible. Therefore the first step must be to synchronize the agents and their positioning systems. However, the environment does not provide a way of doing this in just one step as agents must travel to reach each other at their limited vision distances or employ some sort of environment position recognition.

However, it is not necessary to wait until all the agents in the team are synchronized to perform tasks. Therefore, agents will be divided into synchronized groups which are created naturally as the agents meet and synchronize amongst each other. Within these groups, agents can cooperate. It is also useful to check that agents are not planning to perform certain actions that would lead to conflict and unsuccessful action result. Therefore, within each group, all actions which can create conflict will first have to be approved by the group's reservation system.

Planning of actions that will lead to the completion of tasks can be done within groups. However, the agent should still be able to plan its own actions. Moreover, due to the dynamics of the environment, plans may not be up-to-date or applicable after only one simulation step. Therefore, group and local planning at every step seems to be the most appropriate way. Planning is divided into several levels. First, high-level goals, which we call options, will be calculated. Based on these options, goals and plans will be generated. The agent then selects a plan according to predetermined priorities and submits it to the reservation system. If a plan is approved by the reservation system, then agents submit the first action of the plan as their action for the current step. This will lead to our agents being reactive, but at the same time fulfilling the planned tasks and cooperating with other agents.

The whole synchronisation work is centralised. There is a register class for this purpose. The agents will send their report at each step and it will evaluate and inform group managers accordingly. Main function of the agent's report is letting the Register class know that agent has finished evaluating percepts and his map is up to date with current step.

The previous paragraph described the basic ideas of the strategy that was used to control the agents in this contest. For better clarity, the sequence diagram of one step in the simulation is shown in Fig. 1. The following subsections will describe each part of the strategy in more detail.

2.2 Synchronization

Agent synchronization is essential in this contest. As already addressed, agents do not know their absolute position on the environment grid. Hence, they are not even able to simply deduce each other's relative difference. So without synchronisation, no meaningful group actions can be planned. Agents cannot even pass map information to each other as not to explore the same very recently already explored cells.

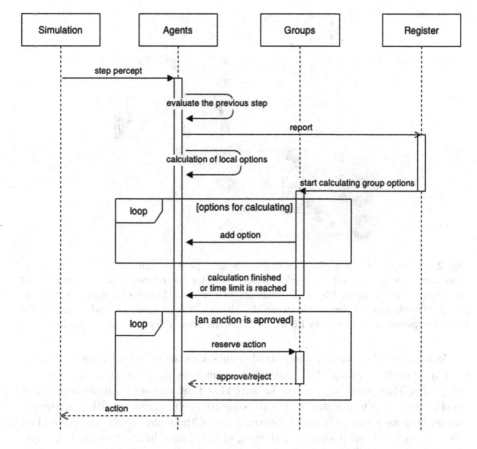

Fig. 1. Sequence diagram of one step in the simulation.

However, there are several aspects in the scenario that we can use to synchronize the agents. All agents have the same order of the coordinate axes. The agent in step perception sees other agents and knows their affiliation to the team and relative position to itself. The last and probably most helpful aspect is the fact that agents are not limited in communication in any way.

By combining these aspects, we are already able to get enough information to synchronize the agents. By exchanging messages, agents can compare their perceptions. If two agents see other agent at the same distance but in the opposite direction, and no other agent sees another agent at the same distance and direction, the two agents can be sure that they see each other.

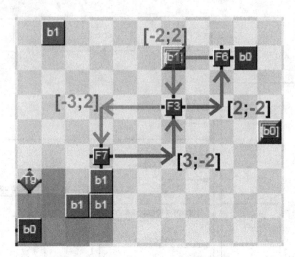

Fig. 2. Example of using distance difference for agent recognition. In this example there are three agents, F3, F6 and F7. Lets consider the situation in the figure from the perspective of agent F3. The difference of positions between it and agent F6 is $[2; -2]$. The distance difference between the objects seen by agent F3 and F7 is $[-3; 2]$. From the perspective of agents F6 and F7, the distance differences are opposite.

As an example, consider one pair of agents. One sees a friendly agent relative to it at position dx, dy. And the other agent sees the first agent at position $-dx$, $-dy$. Then these agents can be sure that they can see each other and can synchronize. This way agent is able to compute their relative position difference and as long as agents maintain a correct log of their movement, they are then able to compute their position for the rest of the simulation. A practical example of agent-relative difference is shown in Fig. 2.

As already mentioned, our strategy is to form synchronized agents into groups. At the beginning of the simulation, n groups are created for n agents (so each agent has its own group). If two agents meet each other and each belongs to a different group, then the two groups can be merged and from now on, all agents from both previous groups are synchronized together.

This synchronization in our system is not performed by the agents themselves, but by the register. Once all agents have submitted their reports, the register builds a set of positions and their corresponding set of agents. If it finds two agents that see each other according to the rule described above, it merges their groups so that agents from one group are added to the second group.

For clarity, this process is demonstrated by Algorithm 1.

Algorithm 1: Synchronization of agents

seeingAgents ← (agentA, agentB, dx_{AB}, dy_{AB}) for all the pairs of agents
who see each other;

foreach *(*agent1, agent2, dx, dy*) in* seeingAgents **do**
    if *there is only one pair (*agent3, agent4, -dx, -dy*)* **then**
        assume that agent1 == agent4 and agent2 == agent3;
        if *the agents are not in the same group* **then**
            add all agents from the second group to the first;
        end
    end
end

2.3 Constructing a Map

The second important aspect that is necessary for proper planning is the creation of an environment map. Each agent starts with their own map. Since the agent does not know its absolute position in the grid, its initial position in its local memory is at position $[0, 0]$. As the agent explores the environment, all objects obtained from percepts are added to its map. A timestamp is also added to these objects and even all history is recorded for sake of additional data compilation and future algorithm expansion possibilities. Since the environment changes frequently, it is necessary to recheck the already discovered cells periodically. Cells with an older timestamp take precedence over those recently discovered when agents are deciding which part of the grid to explore. When exactly specific exploring action is used will be described in more details in Sect. 2.4, but map percepts are recorded throughout all actions and agents.

The previous section described how agents are synchronized. The moment a new agent is added to the group, the map can also be synchronized. Each group has shift vectors stored that determine the shift of the agent's initial position from the group's founder initial coordinate. The group's first agent (agent that was originally in this group by itself) has this vector $[0, 0]$ which means that his map is on the group level interpreted without shift. The difference vector obtained during synchronization is used to compute this vector. The position of the agent is added to the group is first subtracted from this vector. And then the position of the agent who met the new agent is added. This calculates the shift vector, which is then used to synchronize the maps. All members still retain their own maps and in case of critical de-synchronization (some event which results in unexpected and/or unknown coordination shift), an agent can be expelled and his data are automatically no longer used in group map view.

For each round, the group constructs a group map snapshot. It is constructed from the local maps of the agents in the group using shift vectors by adding cells to the group map. If it occurs that there is already a cell at a position in the group map, the one with the newer timestamp will be added. This constructed map is then used for action planning. If two agents report different objects on the same spot at the same time, then both agents are marked for additional investigation. For that reason, their data viewed as unreliable until the problem is resolved.

Handling Grid Looping. In this scenario, constructing the map is more complicated because the grid loops both horizontally and vertically. So if two agents are already synchronized (they are in the same group) and one of them has moved, for example, off the left edge of the map then it will appear on the right side. If the agent meets the other agent again their distance difference will not match.

Unfortunately, we have found no other way to determine if this situation has happened other than when the agents meet again as at that point it is no longer possible to find out exactly where the edge of the map is. But we can at least estimate the size of the map.

Ideally, the agent would be able to recognize on its own (or with the help of a group map) that it is in a different location on the map. However, we consider this to be impossible due to the dynamics of the environment and could also be unreliable in the case of maps with repeating patterns.

Algorithm 2: The principle of finding the map edges

---

limitX ← null;
limitY ← null;

if *agents* agent1 *and* agent2 *have different distance differences to each other* **then**
    loopPoint ← (agent1.position - agent2.position) - distanceDifference;
    if loopPoint.$x \neq 0$ **then**
        newLimitX ← |loopPoint.x| ;
        if limitX $==$ *null* **then**
         | limitX ← newLimitX;
        else if limitX $\neq$ newLimitX **then**
         | limitX ← min(limitX, newLimitX, abs(newLimitX- limitX));
    end
    do the same for position Y;
end

The principle of our edge finding method is shown in Algorithm 2. At the beginning of the simulation, the edges of the map are unknown. The agents explore the environment, and if they meet again and their distance difference vectors are not as expected, we know that one of them has crossed a map edge at least once. Now we can arbitrarily assign the edge and calculate how many times agents have crossed it.

For the calculation, we use an auxiliary point, which we called *loopPoint*. This point is computed as the difference of the agent's positions and the difference of the distance difference vectors. If one of the coordinates is 0, we know that the agent has not crossed the map's edge in this axis (or both agents have crossed it the same number of times). If the edge has not yet been found, the coordinates of this auxiliary point will be used as the new point representing map length. Otherwise, the map length is set as the minimum of the old value, new value or the positive remainder of their difference. (This efficiently detects the size of the map, in cases such as if the first point was found after three border crossing and the second meeting point after two.)

In our system, this logic is implemented in the same section as agent synchronization. Thus, the edge computation is taken care of by the register when it receives reports from all agents. If the register finds unexpected distance difference vectors during agent synchronization, it calculates an auxiliary point and stores it in a separate list. After synchronization is complete, all these points are processed.

The found edge (limit) is then used to calculate the position in the map using the modulo operation. In case when the coordinate is less than 0, the found limit is added to its value. In this way, if the agent has crossed the edge, we can obtain its correct distance to other objects on the map.

2.4   Agent Reasoning Cycle

In the agent's reasoning cycle, for each step of the simulation, the previous action is evaluated (for example, updating the map or changing the position on the map in case of movement) and the action for the current simulation step is selected. In Sect. 2.1 describing the strategy, we stated that since the environment is highly dynamic, planning at the local and group level should be done for each step of the simulation.

Last year, we already introduced a system of options. Each option represents an option available to the agent at the current step. Their computation takes place both at the local level, where the agent considers its options given its capabilities and the information in the local map, and at the group level. To calculate the group options, a group map is constructed as described in Sect. 2.3.

Agents have to perform an action within a limited time, if they do not, they would needlessly lose that action and the enemy team would gain an advantage. For this reason, the actions are calculated in a predetermined order. During the calculations, the watchdog monitors the time and if the calculation takes too long it will stop calculating more possible actions and the agent will have to choose from those actions that have managed to be calculated within the time limit. The options and their order of calculation are shown in Fig. 3.

Local options calculation is computationally less demanding, there are the following five local options in our system:

- *Dodge* it is one of the simplest options, it will check if it is necessary to perform an evasive maneuver. For example, when an agent or some attached block is occupying space with a clearing marker, the agent has to find the shortest path to safety. This action is intended to protect an agent's integrity, especially when it is carrying blocks.

Calculation of agent options

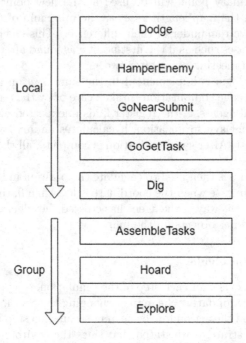

Fig. 3. Order of calculating of agent options.

- *HamperEnemy* is another simple option as it only checks immediate vicinity for enemy agents and creates clearing action on their position.
- *GoNearSubmit* finds the nearest goal cell and the path to it. This option intends to bring agents close to submit areas to reduce their collective distance difference and possibly to find other friendly agents to enable synchronization on a larger scale.
- *GoGetTask* is the most complicated local option. If the agent has no assigned (and current) task and carries some blocks, it tries to find a task for which it has the most potential. If such a task is found it then plots the path to the nearest task board.
- *Dig* finds a way to the nearest terrain and, if in range, performs a clear action. This is intended as a last resort in case the agent is blocked by terrain and does not know the way to any useful location.

The purpose of the *Dodge* and *HamperEnemy* options is clear for competitive or hazardous environment. The *GoGetTask* option is essential for fulfilling tasks and earning points in the contest. Whereas the *GoNearSubmit* and *Dig* options are intended as backup options if there is a problem with pathfinding or a group event planning.

Group options calculation starts when the last agent sends its report. This report is sent when the agent evaluates the previous action. There are three group options:

- *AssembleTasks* searches for blocks and paths for active tasks.
- *Hoard* option is designed for getting blocks (both existing in the environment and requesting new blocks from dispensers) and attaching them the agent's body. This option is very important because, as already mentioned, agents assemble structures to complete a task only from those blocks that are already attached to an agent.
- *Explore* sends agents to explore unknown or long-unvisited parts of the environment. The goal of this option is to discover new goal cells, dispensers, task boards, blocks and other agents. The unexplored area is divided among the agents and each agent explores its assigned part of the environment. This is usually the area to which the agent is closest. If there are no unexplored parts in the map, the parts that have been unvisited for the longest time will be explored again.

The most important option in terms of earning points is *AssebleTasks*. This option is also very computationally intensive, but if the other two options are not calculated, it is not as critical a situation as if this option had not been calculated.

2.5 Goals and Plans

Our agents have one persistent goal and that is to collect as many points as possible by completing tasks. In the previous section we described the system of options. These options are in fact sub-goals of the mentioned persistent goal. For these goals, plans are created in the form of a stack of actions during the calculation of options. These actions correspond to the actions available to agents in the contest.

The names of the plans usually correspond to the goals for which they were created. The exception is the *AssembleTasks* goal/option, for which *GoConnect* and *GoSubmit* plans can be created. A *Roam* plan is created for the *Explore* target. There is also a *Split* plan that is created immediately as the connect action is successfully executed.

The plan to be executed is selected according to its priority, the order of the plans by priority is shown in Fig. 4.

The plan with the highest priority is *GoSubmit* and is adopted when an agent is able to submit a task by the blocks it has attached to its body. If no task can be submitted and the agent is connected to another agent, it will choose to execute the *Split* plan. This ordering is intended to eliminate unintentional changes in the position of agents that drag each other by movement actions.

Next in the order is the *GoSubmit* plan again, but only if the length of the plan is less than 3. In this case, this plan is preferred over the *Dodge* plan. The reason for this order is that the submission of tasks can probably be completed

Agent plan selection

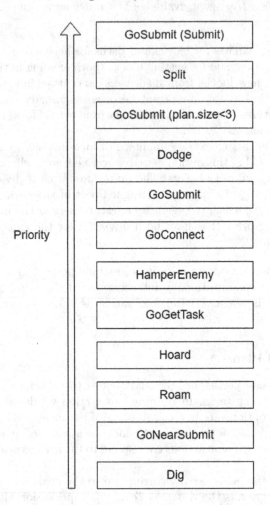

GoSubmit (Submit)
Split
GoSubmit (plan.size<3)
Dodge
GoSubmit
GoConnect
HamperEnemy
GoGetTask
Hoard
Roam
GoNearSubmit
Dig

Priority

Fig. 4. Priority order of plan selection.

before the clear action is performed. Which is more advantageous for the agent. If there is more than one movement action in the plan, it will be executed after the dodge plan.

Then follows the rest of *GoSubmit* and *GoConnect* plans and only if none of the above plans are possible, then there is selection of *HamperEnemy* plan. By trial and error, we found this order most effective as increasing the priority of *HamperEnemy* leads to our agents too often chasing enemy agents and not scoring enough points.

If none of the plans described above is available or executable, the rest of the plans are selected in the order shown in Fig. 4. In fact, there also a one *DoNothing* plan at the top and also the bottom of priority order. However, this plan is only used when the agent is disabled (the top order one) or when the agent has no other action available to perform, so it was not included in the order among the other plans.

As already mentioned, the agent must have certain actions approved by the reservation system before the action is taken to avoid collision with other agents. For this reason, new plans are created even when higher priority plans are already present. These plans have to be approved by the reservation system in their entirety (or reasonable length in case of a very long plans), if the reservation system finds any conflicts with plans from the other agents, plan will be rejected and other plan has to be selected. After the reservation system approves a plan, the first action is selected by the agent for the execution.

Finding the suitable structures for task selection and submission is a crucial part of our system. Assembling these parts is only possible with the cooperation of multiple agents who already have some blocks attached to their body. The finding of suitable structures and the creation of sub-goals is performed within the *AssembleTasks* option calculation in the following steps:

1. Insert all agents into Connection Candidates Set (CCS).
2. If an agent already carries a structure to complete a task and is able to plot a path to a goal area, create a new *Submit* plan for this agent and remove it from the CSS.
3. Sort the structures carried by the agents in order from most complete to least complete and relative to the value of the task.
4. For all active tasks and all agents in the CSS, generate combinations of agent pairs and structures that fulfil a task, respecting the order from the previous step. All generated combinations must be connected and must not overlap in any block.
5. Sort the generated structures according to the steps needed to assemble them and the reward for the corresponding task.
6. While there is a suitable pair of agents in CSS to join their blocks into a structure:
   - Select a generated structure according to the order from the previous step for which both agents are in CSS.
   - Create corresponding *GoConnection* plans for these agents.
   - Remove these agents from CCS.

Generating a combination for each task, each agent, and each block would be very resource intensive, so sorting and option pool trimming is implemented in multiple places in the algorithm.

2.6 Action Reservation System

As mentioned in the section describing the strategy and in the previous section, an action must be approved by the reservation system before it can be executed.

Each group has its own reservation system. Its principle is simple. The reservation system creates a map that represents the expected environment in future steps. When an agent is selecting its intended plan, the reservation system tries to insert the intended changes for every step into the map of that future step. If there are no collisions, the plan and its first action can be approved. However, if there is a collision, the plan is rejected and the agent must choose another plan.

The principle will be demonstrated with an example for clarity. Since this system was carried over from last year's system, the logs from last year's contest, shown in Fig. 5, will be used as an example.

```
7                                    7      b1 b1 3

b1                          X        b1                        X
```

      (a) Agent 7 reserving block request.   (b) Agent 3 reserving step to the right.

```
.  .  .  .  .  .  .  b0 M  .  .  .        .  .  .  b0 F  .  .  .  .  .
.  .  .  .  .  .  .  .  .  .  .  .        .  .  .  .  .  .  .  .  .  .
.  .  .  .  .  .  .  .  M  .  .           .  .  .  .  .  .  .  M  M  .
.  .  7  b1 b1 3  .  .  M  M  M  .        .  .  F  .  b1 b1 3  .  M  M  M  M
.  .  D  .  .  .  .  .  M  X  .           .  .  b1D .  .  .  .  .  M  XM .
.  .  .  .  .  .  D  .  .  .  .           .  .  .  .  .  .  .  D  .  .  .  .
.  .  .  .  .  .  .  .  .  .  .           .  .  .  .  .  .  .  .  .  .  .
.  .  .  .  .  .  .  .  .  .  .           .  .  .  .  .  .  .  .  .  .  .
```

        (c) Initial step state.   (d) Resulting next step.

Fig. 5. An example of a successful actions reservation. Agents are represented by their numbers. If the map is shown from the perspective of one agent, other friendly agents may be represented by F. The dispenser is represented by D, the block by b and its type. Map origin point is denoted by X and marker cell by M.

This example starts in a situation where two agents with numbers 3 and 7 successfully join blocks in a structure and are disconnected. Agent 7 wants to reserve an action to request a new block from dispenser below (Fig. 5a). At the same time, agent 3 wants to move right towards some goal area (Fig. 5b). There will be no conflict between these actions and therefore both will be approved. Figure 5c shows the map before executing reserved actions and Fig. 5d at the beginning of the next step.

3   Summary of Matches

This year, in addition to us, four other teams took part in the tournament, and our team played three matches with each of them. We achieved a good result and in the end, to our delight, we won the competition. Of course, not all of our matches were victorious. Out of a total of twelve matches, we won ten, in two cases our opponent won. Our best score was 314 points, which is the second best score played during the tournament. Each of the teams finished the game in at least one case with zero points. In the following paragraphs we will try to summarize the highlights of the individual matches we participated in.

Round 1, Against JaCaMo Builders. Our first opponent was the JaCaMo Builder team. In three games we got full points. In all games, we scored several dozen points, with a low of 38 and a high of 113. Early on, we had connectivity issues and our team was down for the first 120 steps. After that, it was woken up and completed a total of eight tasks. Six of them were two-point tasks where the agent delivered only one block, one task was for eight points where the agent managed to deliver a two-block task and our team received eight points with this. We got the most points, eighteen, with a three-block task, which was our biggest achievement in this game. Here we managed to do what our system is prepared for. Two agents with partial block structures met and learned that they were able to piece together from their parts the structure that is currently required. This too was then delivered to the target area within the time limit. For most of the games, the opponent did not show significant activity to meet the goals.

In the second game, it seemed at first that the opposing team came into the game hard. They performed clear actions on our players, but mostly just to block them and not when our agents were carrying blocks. It also happened that the opposing team's agents would temporarily perform clear actions on our agents, but then they would run away from them, making the clear action meaningless. Our team works the same way as always, agents pick up blocks and wait for an opportunity to either score or connect the block into the desired shape. It is also evident in the game that our agents are accepting many actual tasks. Since there is no penalty for not completing a task, they can afford to do so and it is a rational action on their part. Overall, we scored 113 points in this game, scoring nine times in total. In four cases for a simple two-point task for one block. However, we also managed to construct larger shapes. A total of four times they submitted a shape consisting of three blocks and once even a four-block shape for 29 points. This was also our team's highest scoring achievement in this game. The opponent was able to tackle the task at the beginning of the third hundred steps when he handed in a two-block shape for eight points.

The third game took place in a similar way and brought nothing new. The opponents failed to score, and at certain stages, their agents seemed to be stuck or walking without a goal. Our team scored a total of 98 points, scoring 20 times. On fourteen occasions scoring only two points with one block, the greatest success was scoring a three-block shape for eighteen points, which they did twice.

Round 2, Against MLFC. The next opponent was already known to us from the last year, where it was the winner [2]. The first game against MLFC is more interesting because of what the opponent did than what our team did, which was unable to score. Probably in this case the right circumstances did not occur or there was some mis-synchronization and our team was not able to score in either case. The opponent did not attack us and there were no interventions that would have prevented us from scoring. Watching the opponent line up around the crease with individual blocks as team members stacked them up and submit them was entertaining. Everything was going smoothly on their part until step 610, when all the reps who were previously ready to set up their assignments started acting strangely, leaving their blocks, taking obvious actions, and scattering to the surrounding area. Otherwise, however, their team seemed very organized, which in this case led to their victory. However, we will comment on the level of organization and the degree of independence of the agents later in the tournament summary. The match meant our loss and the score was 0:48 for the opposing team.

We then won our next two games against the MLFC team. Here again, we will focus on our team. The second game started more briskly with our team trying to grab some blocks right from the start. Neither team attacked the clear actions of the opponent. Almost all the time our team scored, mostly single blocks, eight times in total and in four cases double blocks. The agents waited for their opportunity, and only on rare occasions did the blocks come together in the desired shape. All this brought us a total score of 53 points. This game was the most interesting and tightest of all the games we played during the tournament in terms of score development. The opposing team did not get to their strategies until the end but then were able to score often. In this case, we won with luck, and if the game had gone on a few more steps, the opposing team would have been happy with the victory.

The third game was in a similar vein. The opponent failed to score, although he started to form his formation already around step 400. After that, they started to cautiously accept tasks, while ours again accepted tasks quite often. But the opponent failed to score and our team scored a total of 90 points. So again, a little bit of statistics to finish, our team scored a total of eighteen times, but eleven of those times with only one block. Just like the last game against the JaCaMo Bulders, our high was scoring twice with three blocks for eighteen points.

Round 3, Against GOAL-DTU. Our next opponent was the GOAL-DTU team. Another traditional participant of this competition deployed a system similar to the one they used in last year's competition [3]. In the first match, they did better than us. In this case, both teams started to collect blocks. While last year the opponent connected one block on each side of their agents, this year they only connected two blocks opposite each other, i.e. they moved around the area in the shape of satellites. We could only see how the opponent performed the tasks in this first game. The moment they accepted the task, they tried to transport the appropriate blocks to the goal area and connect them there in the desired shape before submitting. This they did quite abundantly and the final score came out in their favour with a ratio of 181:62. The biggest achievement of the opponents was to submit a four-block for 64 points. Our team scored more modestly, mostly for two or eight points, but was also able to submit a four-block shape once, but only for 32 points.

The next two games, however, did not confirm this relatively good score and they did not score in either case. Their agents again made some moves with stuck blocks in the shape of a satellite and shot clear actions without any major effect on our team. Our team scored as usual mostly with one or two block shapes and scored a total of 104 points in the second game. Our best score so far was in the third game against GOAL-DTU, where we were able to deliver assignments for 282 points. Statistically, on thirteen occasions a one-block shape for two points, on twelve occasions a two-block shape for eight points, twice three-block shapes for eighteen points, and then one scoring each for fifteen, twenty-seven, thirty-eight and forty-four points. In the last case, it was a four-block shape.

Round 4, Against LTI-USP. The last opponent was the LTI-USP team. Again, our opponents sporadically tried to use clear actions, probably as a hostile act towards our agents. Again, however, these actions did not have much effect and rather resulted in the opponent's agents shooting their own blocks. Thus, the functioning of our team proceeded as in the previous cases. Agents would pick up blocks and wander around until there was an opportunity to connect blocks with another agent or to hand over blocks to complete a task. Our opponents, as observed, tried to stack tasks up in the target area and hand them off right there. In the first game, they succeeded twice and the two-block tasks earned a total of sixteen points. Our team fared better and scored 185 points thanks to five eighteen-point and two thirty-plus point successes.

The second game was similar and the score 148:10 is also similar to the previous game. The last game with this team and the last game in the whole MAPC was the biggest success for us in terms of the score. While our agents delivered larger than two-block assignments on only seven occasions, and even four-block assignments on three of those occasions, they often completed smaller assignments with one or two blocks. They received 116 points for these easier tasks alone. The remaining points were for the larger tasks, and they scored the most points around the one hundred and thirtieth move, with 46 points for a three-block task.

4   Conclusion

After watching these matches, we drew several conclusions. Firstly, the environment in which they were played this year. It seems that it was not as rugged and the agents did not have to deal with collisions with impassable areas. While the assignment promised that getting out of confined areas would be necessary, this was not the case in the end.

Another interesting thing was that, as far as we could see, no team took advantage of the ability to increase movement speed when multiple agents from the same team were attached to blocks. This seems rational, as organizing and synchronizing agents for this would overall result in delays rather than speeding up task delivery.

Also, in general, agents did not significantly attack other teams. While there were occasional clear actions directed against other agents, this did not produce an effect. Therefore, we could say that the scores in each game were determined by the abilities of the individual teams and not by the level of attacks from the opposing team.

As for our team and the good results it achieved, we would see it in several aspects as follows. First, our agents are more reactive and less social than the agents of other teams were. They do not organize themselves around the target area based on the task at hand, but wait for the opportunity and deliver often simple tasks. Further, they accept all possible tasks and do not decide which one they really mean to complete. This may be against the spirit of the rules, but it shows that if there is no penalty for incomplete tasks, then there is no reason not to accept the task. They also took advantage of the fact that to complete a task, it was not necessary to submit the exact shape required, but additional blocks could be attached to that shape, which then dropped off on their own after the required shape was delivered.

Overall, all the teams were able to perform the task and the outcome often depended on luck. We conclude, however, that even less organized groups of multiple independent agents are capable of performing tasks in a dynamic multi-agent environment, and that for some cases such multi-agent system design can yield an efficient and rational system.

5   Limitations and Possible Improvements

Our map coordination system was taken from last year solution and adapted to accommodate basic needs for the looping environment. While mostly working, this adaptation produces occasional errors while handling agents with attached blocks in certain locations. Unfortunately, we were unable to find the source of this error and it is suggested to revise the coordination system from the ground up to better handle looping maps.

Acknowledgment. This work was supported by the project IT4IXS: IT4Innovations Excellence in Science project (LQ1602).

A   Team Overview: Short Answers

A.1   Participants and Their Background

What was your motivation to participate in the contest?
    Our group is related to artificial agents and multi-agent systems, and we wanted to compete in an international contest to test our skills. Last year we took second place, this year we wanted to achieve the same or better result.

What is the history of your group? (course project, thesis, ...)

Members of our research group have been teaching artificial intelligence at our faculty for nearly 20 years. Most of the projects or theses in our group concern the topic of artificial intelligence, multi-agent systems, soft-computing and machine learning.

What is your field of research? Which work therein is related?

Vaclav Uhlir: Ecosystems involving autonomous units (mainly autonomous cars).

František Zboril: Artificial agents, BDI agents and prototyping of wireless sensor networks using mobile agents.

František Vidensky: BDI agents (mainly intention/action selection problems).

A.2   Statistics

Did you start your agent team from scratch or did you build on your own or someone else's agents (e.g. from last year)?

Our system is built on the system we developed last year.

How much time did you invest in the contest (for programming, organizing your group, other)?

About 10 h of planning and organizing, 20 h of implementing new features and roughly 100 h of bug hunting.

How was the time (roughly) distributed over the months before the contest?

Due to the other unrelated time constrains our work was mainly done in weeks just before contest.

How many lines of code did you produce for your final agent team?

7461 lines of code (about 5000 of them from were from last year)

1273 comment lines (797 from last year)

59 still active "TODO's" (last year we had 42 left)

How many people were involved?

3

When did you start working on your agents?

We used our system from contest year 2019 and mainly did only adaptation for new system changes and improvements in agents performances.

A.3   Technology and Techniques

Did you make use of agent technology/AOSE methods or tools? What were your experiences?

Agent programming languages and/or frameworks?

No

Methodologies (e.g. Prometheus)?
No

Notation (e.g. Agent UML)?
No

Coordination mechanisms (e.g. protocols, games, ...)?
No

Other (methods/concepts/tools)?
Our agents are in some ways similar to BDI agents but they also use the idea of hierarchical models of behavior. They have their own plans, but at the same time they have to fulfill plans that were planned centrally.

A.4   Agent System Details

How do your agents decide what to do?
Agents are divided into synchronized groups and those groups create plans that are assigned to individual agents. Simultaneously, agents can create some simple plans themselves (for example, clear actions). Resulting plan is then selected for fulfillment by the agent according to priorities and (non)conflicts in group.

How do your agents decide how to do it?
Agents only decide what to do based on ability to do it so they generate all reasonable possibilities of actions resulting in achievement of some goal.

How does the team work together? (i.e. coordination, information sharing, ...) How decentralised is your approach?
Our approach for higher functions is strongly centralized and agents wait for group decision which is triggered by the slowest agent in the group. Individual agents are capable of communicating with the system and by themselves only performing simple tasks (like digging, exploring or attacking enemies).

Do your agents make use of the following features: Planning, Learning, Organisations, Norms? If so, please elaborate briefly.
Our agents are creating plans, but those plans are mainly used for avoiding future conflicts and only one step of the plan is actually used before new plan is generated.

Can your agents change their general behavior during runtime? If so, what triggers the changes?
New plans for agents are generated for each simulation cycle. So every action is dependent only on the current state of the environment. From macro perspective behavioral changes can be observed upon system changes (like sudden availability of new tasks) of when agent experiences desynchronization and will perform only simple tasks (see answer for de/centralization question).

Did you have to make changes to the team (e.g. fix critical bugs) during the contest?

Yes, due to connection issues we had to modify our run cycle and we discovered bug in one of our routines allowing us to increase performance between first and second day of contest.

How did you go about debugging your system? What kinds of measures could improve your debugging experience?

We have custom logging system allowing us to review most of the performed actions and decisions. Unsolved issues remained with identifying actual step in simulation (packaging or marking percepts and actions with step number would solve most of the issues we had in debugging).

During the contest you were not allowed to watch the matches. How did you understand what your team of agents was doing?

We implemented status line where for every step we had step number, our score and counter for each type of plan agents where performing. So we could see for example that 6 agents were working on connecting blocks and just be anticipating every next step where only 4 agents would be connecting and 1 would be carrying objective to the submit area.

Did you invest time in making your agents more robust/fault-tolerant? How?

Yes, in a case of desynchronization with others agents from a group or for agents with conflicting information - those agents where banned from group decisions and where effectively assigned to clearing out terrain and harassing enemy.

A.5   Scenario and Strategy

What is the main strategy of your agent team?

Aiming for closest achievable and possibly high valued tasks.

Please explain whether you think you came up with a good strategy or you rather enabled your agents to find the best strategy.

We think we came up with a good strategy. Our strategy was already tested last year and has been improved this year.

Did you implement any strategy that tries to interfere with your opponents?

Yes, we did. Desynchronized agents or "bored" agents (with low priority plans) could sabotage the opponent's agents by attacking them or their blocks.

How do your agents decide which tasks to complete?

Agents selected task based on mach with currently already held blocks.

How do your agents coordinate assembling and delivering a structure for a task?
In group decision process agents are assigned meeting coordinates. But mainly it can be viewed as "master" agent acquiring task and using "slave" agents to connect other blocks before master goes to submit finished task.

Which aspect(s) of the scenario did you find particularly challenging?
Adapting existing engine to the cyclic map proved to be far more challenging then we expected (this was due to large number and types of access and to internal grid coordination system).

A.6   And the Moral of it is ...

What did you learn from participating in the contest?
A relatively simply looking scenario can present a far greater challenge than expected.

What advice would you give to yourself before the contest/another team wanting to participate in the next?
Start implementing as soon as possible. Create small functioning iterations and let them play against each other to see what and how much improves overall behaviour.

What are the strong and weak points of your team?
Our team has expertise in multiple different languages and coding approach techniques and mainly in rapid development using whatever means necessary. Unfortunately this has begun to be known and members of our team are used for other tasks limiting their time availability.

Where did you benefit from your chosen programming language, methodology, tools, and algorithms?
Good ratio between development speed and performance.

Which problems did you encounter because of your chosen technologies?
Java stack trace bug hunting and git server fault - unexpectedly disabling team synchronization.

Did you encounter previously unseen problems/bugs during the contest?
Yes, percepts decoding became far more unpredictable and harder to manage. (Sometimes steps percepts would be incomplete or missing entirely for some agent.)

Did playing against other agent teams bring about new insights on your own agents?
Not especially.

What would you improve (wrt. your agents) if you wanted to participate in the same contest a week from now (or next year)?
Internal grid system, desynchronization management (with recovery options) and implementing agent mobility update.

Which aspect of your team cost you the most time?
Bug hunting problems inherited from last year.

What can be improved regarding the contest/scenario for next year?
Running matches in virtual environment on server and in repeated rounds in span of weeks.

Why did your team perform as it did? Why did the other teams perform better/worse than you did?
We think our agent are more versatile in having ability to immediately adapt to changing conditions, but this will be better assessed after release of all papers from contest participants.

If you participated in the "free-for-all" event after the contest, did you learn anything new about your agents from that?
Yes, in that scenario our agents where effectively outnumbered by enemy agents so strategy of investing one agent to harass one enemy is no longer effective.

References

1. Brooks, R.: A robust layered control system for a mobile robot. IEEE J. Robot. Autom. **2**(1), 14–23 (1986). https://doi.org/10.1109/JRA.1986.1087032
2. Cardoso, R.C., Ferrando, A., Papacchini, F.: LFC: combining autonomous agents and automated planning in the multi-agent programming contest. In: Ahlbrecht, T., Dix, J., Fiekas, N., Krausburg, T. (eds.) MAPC 2019. LNCS (LNAI), vol. 12381, pp. 31–58. Springer, Cham (2020). https://doi.org/10.1007/978-3-030-59299-8_2
3. Jensen, A.B., Villadsen, J.: GOAL-DTU: development of distributed intelligence for the multi-agent programming contest. In: Ahlbrecht, T., Dix, J., Fiekas, N., Krausburg, T. (eds.) MAPC 2019. LNCS (LNAI), vol. 12381, pp. 79–105. Springer, Cham (2020). https://doi.org/10.1007/978-3-030-59299-8_4
4. Rao, A.S., Georgeff, M.P., et al.: BDI agents: from theory to practice. In: ICMAS, vol. 95, pp. 312–319 (1995)
5. Uhlir, V., Zboril, F., Vidensky, F.: Multi-agent programming contest 2019 FIT BUT team solution. In: Ahlbrecht, T., Dix, J., Fiekas, N., Krausburg, T. (eds.) MAPC 2019. LNCS (LNAI), vol. 12381, pp. 59–78. Springer, Cham (2020). https://doi.org/10.1007/978-3-030-59299-8_3

The 15th Edition of the Multi-Agent Programming Contest - The GOAL-DTU Team

Alexander Birch Jensen⬤, Jørgen Villadsen(✉)⬤, Jonas Weile,
and Erik Kristian Gylling

Algorithms, Logic and Graphs Section, Department of Applied Mathematics
and Computer Science, Technical University of Denmark, Richard Petersens Plads,
Building 324, 2800 Kongens Lyngby, Denmark
jovi@dtu.dk

Abstract. We provide an overview of the GOAL-DTU system for the Multi-Agent Programming Contest, including the overall strategy and how the system is designed to apply this strategy. Our agents are implemented using the GOAL programming language. We evaluate the performance of our agents in the contest and, finally, we discuss how to improve the system based on an analysis of its strengths and weaknesses.

1 Introduction

In 2020/2021 we participated as the GOAL-DTU team in the annual Multi-Agent Programming Contest (MAPC). We are using the GOAL agent programming language [1–4] and we are affiliated with the Technical University of Denmark (DTU). We participated in the contest in 2009 and 2010 as the Jason-DTU team [5,6], in 2011 and 2012 as the Python-DTU team [7,8], in 2013 and 2014 as the GOAL-DTU team [9], in 2015/2016 as the Python-DTU team [10], in 2017 and 2018 as the Jason-DTU team [11,12] and in 2019 as the GOAL-DTU team [13].

In 2020/2021 we had the *Agents Assemble II* scenario; this scenario expands upon the *Agents Assemble* scenario used in the 2019 contest. The *Agents Assemble II* scenario is a highly dynamic environment. The simulations used for the competition usually have a large number of agents that can move freely and even cause changes to the environment, which further adds to its complexity. As a new feature from the previous iteration, when an agent crosses the boundary of the map it will instantly reappear on the opposite side. This transition appears seamless to the agent and no triggers can be perceived. From the points of view of agents, the map may appear to be infinite while, in reality, all maps have finite dimensions. This means that agents may observe already known objects but consider them to be new knowledge. Most agents can usually be observed carrying blocks around the environment while clearing passages to enable their movement. Furthermore, random clear events may occur sporadically. As opposed to the clear actions of agents, which merely remove obstacles, the random clear

© Springer Nature Switzerland AG 2021
T. Ahlbrecht et al. (Eds.): MAPC 2021, LNAI 12947, pp. 46–81, 2021.
https://doi.org/10.1007/978-3-030-88549-6_3

events will both remove and add blocks in an area. Consequently, these random events can rapidly change the environment.

A key characteristic of our agent system is that agents share the same code base and knowledge. As such, the system has a single, universal type of agent. However, the agents still exhibit different behaviours at execution time, as the behaviour of an agent is determined by both its knowledge as well as its current beliefs and goals; these factors dictate the flow of the agent through logic rules and modules.

The paper is organized as follows:

- Section 2 covers the overall strategy of our agents.
- Section 3 describes the knowledge our agents acquire from the environment.
- Section 4 describes the movement of our agents.
- Section 5 describes how our agents communicate.
- Section 6 covers how our agents complete selected tasks.
- Section 7 evaluates our agents' performance in the contest.
- Section 8 discusses improvements to our agent system.
- Section 9 makes some concluding remarks.

We assume basic knowledge of the GOAL agent programming language [1–4]. Agents in GOAL are self-controlled independent entities, each interacting with the environment and communicating with other agents. The environment is continuously perceived to update each agent's mental state: its beliefs about the current state of affairs and its current goals. A mental state is implemented as a Prolog knowledge base. Rule-based decision-making enables each agent to continuously select an action based on its current mental state. GOAL advocates that agents are programmed to react to changes in their environment rather than executing predetermined plans. Such a reactive approach is not flawless either: it can be difficult for programmers to come up with logical rules that produce the desired behavior. However, overcoming this challenge often produces more flexible agents.

2   The Strategy of Our Agents

The main strategy of our agents is both proactive and reactive: agents explore the map to gather information and collect blocks while reacting to obstacles they meet along their way. Our agents employ an A* path finding algorithm to optimize short-term movement. Agents compose plans to solve available tasks that describe how patterns are to be aligned.

The logic of our strategy is implemented in GOAL in the so-called *main-module*. Here, the GOAL agent selects an action based on its knowledge, beliefs and goals, according to a prioritized list of predefined logic rules.

At the top-level, the strategy of agents is divided into two sub-strategies: exploration and task-solving. The only exception is a special task master agent that delegates tasks. This will be discussed in more detail in Sect. 6. We can consider the two sub-strategies to be the roots of a hierarchical goal network. Each of these goals branches into sub-goals that need to be achieved in order to complete the higher-level goal. Consider as an example a goal of solving a task. In order to achieve this goal, we first need to find and attach blocks needed for the task pattern before the pattern can be assembled and submitted. Each of these sub-tasks corresponds to sub-goals of the high-level goal of completing the task.

In the following section we will treat each of our two sub-strategies separately. We provide descriptions of the implemented agent logic below.

2.1   Exploration of the Map

Initially, all of our agents will act upon their initial goal to explore the map. This has two main purposes: to cover as much of the map as possible and to search for blocks or dispensers. When an agent locates a block or dispenser, it will attempt to attach two blocks on opposite sides; this in order to minimize the negative effect on maneuverability of carrying blocks. The mechanics of exploration is further explained in Sect. 4.

In the following, an action is selected based on the first applicable rule:

- If the agent does not have two blocks attached (which should be attached to opposite sides of the agent) and there is a block or dispenser within the field of vision of the agent:
  - If the agent is next to the block/dispenser, but it needs to rotate in order to attach a block:
    - If it is possible for the agent to rotate, then rotate.
    - If the agent can move in some direction, then move.
  - If the agent is next to a block, then attach the block.
  - If the agent is next to a dispenser, then request a block from that dispenser.
  - If the agent can move towards the block/dispenser, then move.
- If there is a good direction for the agent to move and explore, then move.
- If there are no other good options for the agent, then skip.

Note that agents sometimes move in a random direction if they are next to a block/dispenser and are required to rotate. The idea is that often just a few moves enable the agent to perform the rotation.

2.2   Accepting and Submitting Tasks

The win condition for the scenario is to score the most points. Points are gained by accepting tasks (at task boards) and submitting the required pattern. The currently available tasks are always perceivable by the agents. Based on the currently collected blocks, and information about potentially collected blocks (via block dispensers), we are able to compose so-called task plans. These delegate sub-tasks to each agent required to ultimately submit the pattern and score points.

Task plans are created by a single agent that has the task master role. A task plan delegates to the other agents the gathering and delivery of the required blocks. One of these agents is then selected to have the submit agent role: the agent that submits the pattern and completes the task once the pattern is assembled. All of this is explained more thoroughly in Sect. 6.1.

In the following scenarios, an action is selected based on the first applicable rule, if the current step in the task plan is to gather blocks required for a task:

- If the agent does not have room for the (maximum two) blocks we should deliver, then detach a block.
- If there is a dispenser or block of the required type within the agent's field of view:
  - If the agent is next to the object of interest, but it needs to rotate in order to attach the object:
    - If it is possible for the agent to rotate, then rotate.
    - If the agent can move in some direction, then move.
  - If the agent is next to a block, then attach the block.
  - If the agent is next to a dispenser, then request a block from that dispenser.
  - If the agent can move towards the object of interest, then move.
- If true then move towards the dispenser from the plan.

In the following scenarios, an action is selected based on the first applicable rule, if the current step in the task plan is to get to a task board:

- If the agent has a block attached that is not included in the plan and the agent needs space to attach a block included in the plan, then detach the block not included in the plan.
- If the agent is within a distance of two cells from the task board, then accept the task from the plan.
- If true then move towards the task board.

In the following scenarios, an action is selected based on the first applicable rule, if the current step in the task plan is to get to the specified goal cell and submit the task:

- If the agent is the submit agent:
  - If the pattern is blocked by an agent from the opposing team, try to perform a clear action on that agent.
  - If the agent is at the specified goal cell:
    - If the agent can submit the task, then submit the task.
    - If the agent can connect to a block in the task pattern, then connect to the block.
    - If the agent is in position and is simply waiting for other agents, and there are agents from the opposing team nearby, try to perform a clear action on one of them.
    - If the agent is in position, then skip.
    - If the agent needs to rotate, and it is possible, rotate.
  - If true, move towards the goal cell.
- If the agent is not the submit agent:

- If the agent has connected a block to another block, detach it.
- If a block/obstacle is blocking the pattern, then perform a clear action on it.
- If the agent is in position:
  - If the agent can connect a block to the task pattern, then connect the block.
  - If the agent is waiting for other agents:
    - If there are enemy agents nearby, then try to clear them.
    - If true then skip.
  - If rotation is required to connect a block to the task pattern, then rotate.
- If true, then move towards the goal cell.

3 Storing and Maintaining Information

In Sect. 2, we described how our agents operate based on a strategy that is implemented as decision rules. Such decisions are based on the information available to the agents: their mental states. Mental states of agents consist of their current beliefs and goals as well as a knowledge base which contains (static) domain-specific knowledge. All our agents have identical knowledge bases, as all agents are initiated with identical knowledge.

Our GOAL agents connect to the environment using the environment interface standard (EIS) [1]. This interface allows for communication between GOAL and the environment via text messages using the JSON (JavaScript Object Notation) format. A JSON message consists of a collection of name/value pairs. Generally speaking, we maintain the structure of perceived values when storing them as Prolog-like terms in the belief base. In some cases, we expand with additional information that is not made available by the environment, such as the agent's own attached block which can be inferred by the agents.

Because the *Agents Assemble II* scenario features a highly dynamic environment, our agents do not rely on creating a complete representation of their environment—it is almost impossible to maintain an accurate picture. Instead, our agents mostly rely on their current percepts. Agents only perceive objects, including other agents, within a limited field of vision. This field of vision corresponds to a circle in the taxicab geometry, where the radius for the circle is given by the environment, see Fig. 1.

3.1 Immutable Objects in the Environment

The highly dynamic environment implies that information perceived by agents may become outdated quickly. However, there are a number of immutable objects in the environment, namely the block dispensers, goal cells, and task boards. All of these are unaffected by clear actions and are static throughout a simulation. Our agents will therefore permanently store all known positions of these objects in their belief bases. The fact that dispensers, goal cells, and task boards are immutable facilitates our task planning algorithm which is explored further in Sect. 6.1.

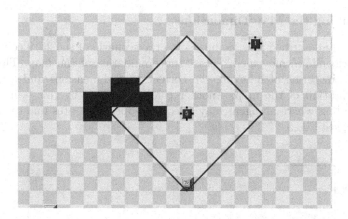

Fig. 1. This figure depicts two agents. The agent in the center of the picture (labeled 5) is surrounded by a blue diamond shape. This shape is a circle of radius five in the taxicab geometry, and it represents the field of vision of the agent. The agent 5 can thus only percept objects within the blue shape, therefore, the two agents in the picture cannot perceive one another. The picture is taken from the monitor that has been developed for the contest. (Color figure online)

Because these immutable objects are static throughout a simulation, we are able to store and share this information amongst our agents without worrying about the information becoming outdated at a later point. The details of agent communication are covered in Sect. 5. In fact, our decentralized planning is only enabled because of our information sharing strategy.

3.2 Agreeing on Coordinates

Each of our agents maintain its own separate coordinate system. The origin of this coordinate system is initialized as the agent's starting position. The separate coordinate systems pose a challenge when agents share information that is relative to their own coordinates. One solution to this problem would be to have agents agree on a single coordinate system. This implies that whenever agents meet and share their relative coordinates, they should decide on a common coordinate system. However, we found that this approach requires extensive protocols to be developed in order to ensure connected agents always agree on the same coordinate system. We have instead employed a solution in which each agent stores the offsets of all other agents. This means that whenever an agent receives information from another agent, the coordinates are easily translated. One drawback to our approach is that agents need to maintain a synchronized data set of offsets amongst all agents to avoid false information (such issues may in turn propagate throughout the execution and cause beliefs to become increasingly out of sync). How agents meet and share their coordinates is explained more thoroughly in Sect. 5.1.

3.3 Inferring the Map Dimensions

We previously described how, compared to the scenario of the 2019 contest, the new scenario allows movement across the boundaries of the map. This poses a challenge in terms of inferring the correct map dimensions and avoiding a misrepresentation of the map. Another challenge posed by this is in relation to path finding where an agent may select sub-optimal routes due to a lack of knowledge, see Fig. 2.

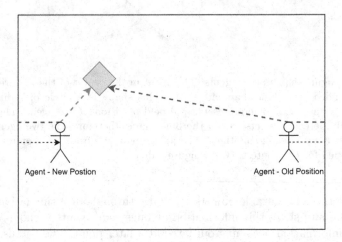

Fig. 2. Here, an agent unknowingly moves across the border of the map and reappears on the other side, represented by the black arrow. Once at the other the side, the agent has to reach the resource represented by the blue rhombus. The agent falsely believes, that the fastest way to reach this resource is by crossing the map again, and will then traverse the entire map. This path is represented by the dashed red line. In reality, the agent is very close to the resource, and the shortest path is shown by the dashed green line. (Color figure online)

To avoid the mentioned misrepresentation of the map, agents employ a strategy that intends to discover, and communicate to other agents, the dimensions of the map. This plays a central role in estimating distances. If the dimensions of the map are inferred, agents may knowingly decide to cross the edges of the map when this is deemed beneficial. Thus, knowing the dimensions of the map not only ensures that the agents do not flood their belief bases with false (or rather, sub-optimal) locations of resources, but also optimizes the agent's movement.

The dimensions of the map are inferred as an agent crosses the map and reappears on the other side, unknowingly. When the agent meets another agent, to which it was connected to prior to crossing the map, it infers the dimensions from the stored agent offsets. If their shared information does not match, it can be deduced that one of the agents must have crossed the map. The map dimensions can then be inferred from this discrepancy and are shared with all other agents.

4   Moving About in the Environment

In the following section, we touch upon the various movement strategies that are employed by our agents, depending on their current goals. The use of movement strategies can generally be divided into two cases: one for general map exploration and one for movement towards a fixed position.

4.1   General Map Exploration

As previously described, all agents are initialized with the goal of exploring the map. Here, an agent's sole purpose is to reach unexplored regions of the map. The efficiency with which any single agent reaches these unexplored regions is considered of low importance. However, we note that a more effective, collective exploration could benefit our system by allowing for a quicker transition to task-solving.

Our design philosophy is that exploration should have a relatively low computational complexity, considering all agents are exploring initially. Furthermore, from last year's competition, we learned that a somewhat random approach to exploration is adequate. We employ a simple pseudo-random heuristic, defined in Eq. 1. The heuristic is based on expected benefits of moving in each possible direction and heavily favors cells that are unexplored. Here, d is the direction being evaluated, ΔS is the number of steps since the cell was visited, and $|\Delta x(d)| + |\Delta y(d)|$ is the Manhattan distance to the cell from the current location of the agent. The direction with the best value is then chosen.

$$h(d) = \sum_{visited} \begin{cases} \dfrac{|\Delta x(d)| + |\Delta y(d)|}{\Delta S^2} & \text{if } |\Delta x(d)| + |\Delta y(d)| \leq 30 \text{ and } \Delta S > 0 \\ 0 & \text{otherwise} \end{cases} \quad (1)$$

Our current implementation does not enable agents to share information about visited cells. We note that doing so could potentially lead to faster and more thorough exploration. This could be particularly beneficial on larger maps.

4.2   Movement Towards a Fixed Position

As explained in Sect. 3, the agents do not maintain a complete representation of the map. Because of this, we cannot rely on classical route planning algorithms. In the previous year's contest, our agents employed a simple heuristic similar to the exploration heuristic to determine a movement in each simulation step. In terms of computational complexity, this is a lightweight solution compared to heavy route planning algorithms and it is easy to implement. However, this naive approach proved to be inefficient in cases where the agent encounters obstacles. We observed that agents would spend a lot of steps trying to get around obstacles and progress was often severely impacted by agents getting stuck.

To circumvent this issue, our current iteration of the system employs a solution that mixes the heuristics-based approach with local route planning. The idea is to get the best of both worlds. In case the agent is moving towards a fixed location, it will thus first generate a move based on the simple movement heuristics. In case the move is constructive (see below), it will simply perform it. Otherwise, the agent will instead resort to route planning within its field of vision. The optimal position in the field of vision, with regard to the target location, is set as a *way point*. The path planning returns a sequence of actions that will enable the agent to reach this way point. The agent will keep progressing through the sequence as long as possible. In case the sequence becomes invalid or the agent reaches its way point, the process starts over: a way point is found, and the agent attempts to generate an action with the simple heuristic, otherwise resorting to route planning. Once the fixed location is within the agent's field of vision, this location will be used as the final way point.

Any move that brings the agent strictly closer to the target position, while avoiding recently visited positions, is considered constructive. We consider a position to be recently visited if it was visited fewer than 3 steps ago. This somewhat remedies situations where the agent might otherwise get caught in dead ends, endlessly moving back and forth without making progress.

Our definition of constructive moves is quite restrictive. For instance, whenever an agent has to go around an obstacle, the move will always be considered nonconstructive. To get the full benefits of the heuristics-based approach, the definition of constructive moves is relaxed. The relaxation involves categorizing all moves immediately next to obstacles as constructive as well. More precisely, if an agent moves along an obstacle that is closer to the target position than the agent, the move is constructive. This means that the agent can move around obstacles without resorting to route planning. However, this may also potentially lead to undesirable situations, as was observed during the competition: if two agents try to move past each other, they could end up moving further away from their respective target positions than desired. This specific problem is illustrated in Fig. 3. This observed problem has us questioning whether the described relaxation has been beneficial or not.

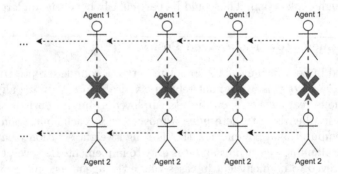

Fig. 3. This figure depicts two agents that wish to pass each other. Agent 2 wishes to go north, and agent 1 wishes to go south. This is not possible though, as the agents are in the way of each other. According to the relaxed heuristic, both agents can move west though. But this will simply bring the agents to the same dilemma once more.

In contrast to last year's implementation, we are now also utilizing the *clear* action with the introduction of local route planning. We expect that agents should no longer get stuck. We also expect general improvements to the efficiency of agent movement.

Route planning is implemented using the A* path finding algorithm. The heuristic used for the A* algorithm is simply the sum of the step cost and the distance to the target position. The search is terminated once a position at the edge of the field of vision is chosen, or if the target position is reached. To ensure effective route planning, the A* algorithm has been implemented in 2 versions. One version does not consider clear actions, and one does. This is due to the extra complexity introduced by the clear action. It was experimentally found that in a lot of cases, searches including clear actions resulted in drastic impacts to the running time. Consequently, our agents first initialize a search without enabling clearing of obstacles. If this is not feasible, the agent skips the current step to focus resources on computing a path that relies on clear actions as well.

5   Communication Between Agents

Solving any task in unison requires communication among agents. Agents need to agree on a task to solve as well as a goal cell at which to deliver the task. They also need to assign the collection and delivery of blocks required to solve it. The challenge is that each agent has its own coordinate system and thus agents cannot communicate about locations on a global level. Therefore, agents must somehow merge their coordinate systems, and this process is what we describe as connecting to other agents. The actual communication itself is facilitated by the extensive communication scheme that is provided by the GOAL agent programming language. The communication features of the GOAL programming language facilitate communication between agents through direct messaging or using channels. In general, the philosophy is to form communication channels instead of direct messaging when multiple agents are involved. As an example, our agents communicate via a channel *explore*, which is created during initialization of the system, where they share information to infer the position of other agents.

5.1   Connecting to Other Agents

For our agents, establishing connections equates to learning the origins of the other agents, thus allowing for translation of coordinates between coordinate systems. As a result, it enables agents to communicate the locations of resources. Agents may establish a connection when they are inside each other's field of vision. Since agents do not know the identities of other agents they encounter, the agents compare other perceivable objects in their (assumed) shared field of vision. This is achieved by the agents broadcasting their current position along with coordinates of the objects within their field of vision. In case another agent identifies the same objects, including the broadcasting agent, the two agents will establish a connection. Once agents are connected, they will start sharing information. Note that agents communicate coordinates relative to their starting position. The agent receiving the information will use stored knowledge about the offset between their starting positions to allow for an efficient translation between coordinates.

Ensuring the Correctness of Connections

It is important to ensure that agents will not mistakenly establish connections with agents which were not encountered. This may happen in rare cases where multiple agents encounter each other with similar objects in the shared field of vision. To remedy this, agents check whether there are multiple identical broadcasts, in which case no connections are established. The fact that multiple agents have similar broadcasts indicates that it will not be possible to distinguish those agents from one another.

A further challenge is imposed by the fact that in GOAL, the delivery of messages is not guaranteed in a certain step; it can merely be assumed that all messages will be delivered eventually. As such, the delay in receiving a message might be longer than a single step which can lead to situations where an agent has not received all broadcasts, and thus cannot ensure that no identical broadcasts are present. In our current implementation, all agents are required to broadcast, even if there are no other agents within its field of vision, in which case an empty broadcast is sent. Thus an agent will have to wait until it has received broadcasts from all other agents, before it establishes any new connections. This means, that there is a delay between encountering agents and establishing connections to these agents.

Connection Networks

Up to this point, we have not yet considered cascading effects when establishing connections. If agents can only connect to other agents within their field of vision, all agents have to encounter each other in order to establish connections between all agents. This is obviously not very efficient, especially for larger maps. In many cases, the system might never reach such a state within the limited time frame of a simulation. We are interested in optimizing this behaviour as our task planning relies on connections being established between agents. Essentially, having connections to other agents simply boils down to agents knowing the starting positions of other agents relative to their own.

To explain the process of connection cascading, consider the situation depicted in Fig. 4. The situation has three different networks of connected agents: the first network is made up of Agent 1, 2 and 3, the second network is made up of Agent 4 and 5, and the final network is just Agent 6. A network of connected agents is a set of agents, each knowing the offset of all other agents in the network. In the depicted situation, encounters between Agent 6 and 3, and Agent 4 and 2 occur simultaneously. As such, there is a possibility to connect the three networks. The challenge is now to ensure that all agents in each network establish connections to all agents of the two other networks. In general, this is achieved by having agents broadcast their connections. This allows an agent to infer the resulting network by combining all new connections and

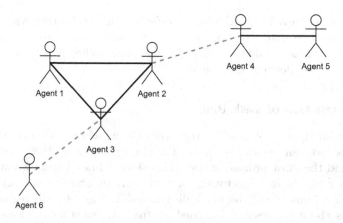

Fig. 4. The figure depicts three existing connection networks symbolised by the solid black lines—one network is the singular agent 6. Two new connections are established: a connection between agent 3 and agent 6, and a connection between agent 2 and agent 4. The resulting network then connects all 6 agents, ensuring that all agents know the offset of all other agents.

existing networks. To optimize the process, only a single agent of each network will compute the resulting network. Once all information necessary to establish new connections has been gathered, said agent will share this information with its own network.

6 Constructing and Executing Task Plans

This section covers how task plans are constructed by the task master and executed by the other agents.

A single agent is dynamically assigned to be *task master*. This agent is responsible for creating task plans and assigning agents to different tasks. The choice of having a single task master is to simplify resource assignment. With just a single agent responsible for computing task plans, we avoid having to deal with mechanisms for ensuring that resources are not allocated for multiple plans by multiple agents—a thread with a single pool of resources makes this much easier to achieve. The main principle of our dynamic task master assignment is to ensure that the chosen task master is connected to the majority of the agents. This is done by delaying the task master assignment to when at least half of the agents in the simulation have connected to each other, as described in Sect. 5.1. Outside of the mentioned delay, we find that the only drawback to our centralisation of task planning is the computational complexity. However, it is not clear if and how this could potentially be improved by parallelization.

The task master keeps track of goal cells and agents that are allocated by the currently active task plans. All cells of a goal zone are considered to be allocated if an active task plan instructs agents to deliver the task in the said goal zone.

The intent is to prevent agents from interfering with each other when solving tasks. However, we note that our current implementation is overly restrictive. One possible solution would be to allow for goal zones to be divided into subareas that may then be allocated individually.

6.1 Construction of Task Plans

Our task planning is initialized by the task master, which orders all the tasks that do not have an active task plan. Tasks are ordered by their reward and deadline, and the most promising task is considered first. The task master will ask all other agents in its network for their current attachments and beliefs about the locations of various block dispensers. The agents will respond with their beliefs about the resources needed for the task, whether the agent knows the location of a task board, and finally an estimated delivery time. The task master collects all responses to see if it is possible to compute a plan. A task describes a specific pattern to complete, and based on the combined resources of the agents, it is possible to search for an assignment of agents to blocks in the pattern which also considers the constraints of the scenario, i.e. how blocks can be attached as well as the positioning of agents for assembling the pattern and submitting it. This assignment delegates specific blocks of the pattern to specific agents and this cannot be changed without dropping the plan completely. While this limitation makes the solution less flexible, we find that the greatest hurdle is to have the agents reach a point where the pattern can be assembled. In case it is not possible to compute a plan, the task master will consider alternative tasks following the task order. In case a plan is created, each agent receives a version of the task plan that is specifically tailored to its perspective: which part of the pattern it should provide, how it should position itself for the assembly, etc.

The task plans delegate the task of submitting to one agent. In doing so, the submitting agent is also instructed to submit the task at a specific goal cell. While the approach has a few drawbacks, there are also several advantages: each agent knows exactly where to deliver its block and agents can easily identify blocks and obstacles to clear that will otherwise obstruct the assembly of the pattern. One drawback is that agents of opposing teams may obstruct the assembly. In this case, our agents will try to perform clear actions on those agents, hopefully leading them to move, but this is not guaranteed to succeed. A better solution would likely be to have a more dynamic approach that uses a fixed goal cell when possible, but with the ability to recompute a new goal cell if needed. As of now, our agents simply give up submitting the task after some time if they fail to make progress.

6.2 Execution of Task Plans

As described above, agents assigned to a task receive a task plan that is local to their perspective. For simplicity, an agent will only be assigned to deliver blocks of a single type. Once assigned to a task, each agent sets out to gather the blocks it is assigned to deliver. The submit agent is also tasked with accepting the task from a task board, as well as submitting the task.

Our agents continuously re-evaluate whether it is still possible to complete the task. For instance, it may happen that an agent loses a block that was to be delivered due to a clear action or event. In such a case, the agent checks if it is possible to re-acquire a block of the required type and deliver it within the deadline. If this is not possible, it will broadcast to the task channel that the task plan should be dropped, at which point all agents are unassigned from the task.

Once the agents are assembled, they will build the pattern outwards from the submit agent. Agents will connect one at a time to the submit agent and then release the corresponding block. If the agent has no more blocks to deliver, it will consider its task as fulfilled and be available to accept other tasks. When the pattern is completed the submit agent will then submit it.

7 Evaluation of Matches

GOAL-DTU competed in four matches against four different opponents in the Multi-Agent Programming Contest of 2020/2021. A match consisted of three simulations, and a simulation started automatically when the previous simulation finished. GOAL-DTU took part in two additional simulations after the contest. In these two simulations, all teams competed against each other.

7.1 GOAL-DTU vs. LTI-USP

LTI-USP allows multiple agents to accept the same task, such that multiple groups of agents could work on the same task. For each task, GOAL-DTU allows only one agent to accept it and only one group of agents to assemble it. Having multiple groups of agents to work on the same task didn't make LTI-USP's agents more effective. It only made their points per resource ratio smaller. It was not the best approach in the second simulation because agents of GOAL-DTU were consistently faster in assembling patterns than LTI-USP's agents. It is shown in Fig. 13 that GOAL-DTU completed more tasks, but it does not show how many of those tasks LTI-USP were trying to complete (Figs. 5, 6, 7, 8, 9, 10, 11, 12, 14, 15, 16, 17, 18 and 19).

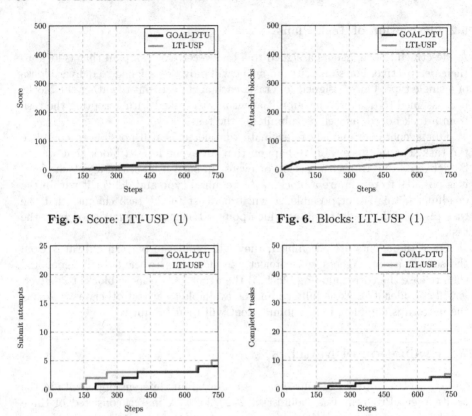

Fig. 5. Score: LTI-USP (1)   **Fig. 6.** Blocks: LTI-USP (1)

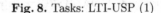

Fig. 7. Submits: LTI-USP (1)   **Fig. 8.** Tasks: LTI-USP (1)

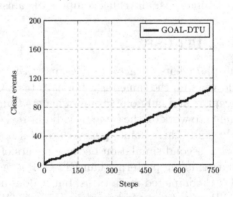

Fig. 9. Clear: LTI-USP (1)

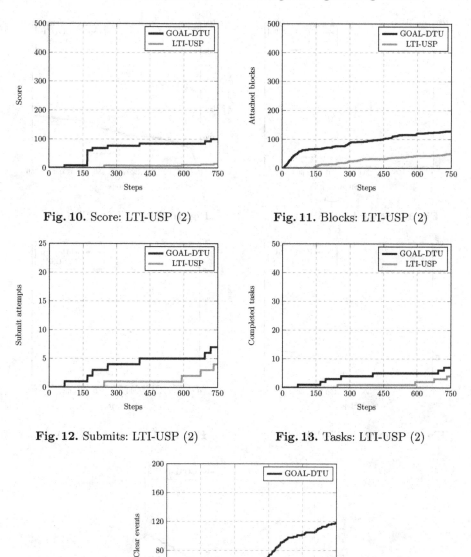

Fig. 10. Score: LTI-USP (2)

Fig. 11. Blocks: LTI-USP (2)

Fig. 12. Submits: LTI-USP (2)

Fig. 13. Tasks: LTI-USP (2)

Fig. 14. Clear: LTI-USP (2)

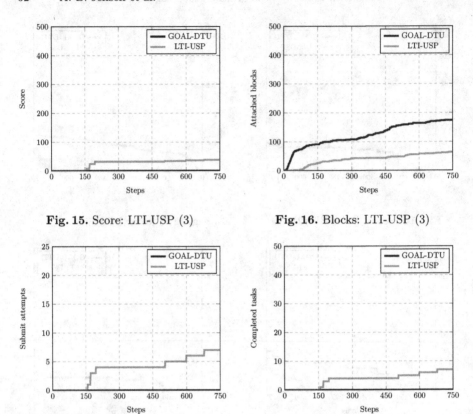

Fig. 15. Score: LTI-USP (3)   **Fig. 16.** Blocks: LTI-USP (3)

Fig. 17. Submits: LTI-USP (3)   **Fig. 18.** Tasks: LTI-USP (3)

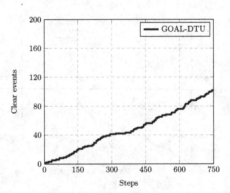

Fig. 19. Clear: LTI-USP (3)

GOAL-DTU had some problems throughout the simulations. The agents moved in each other's way, and sometimes clusters formed. We suspect a minor bug in the explore algorithm is causing agents to move towards each other. The intention is for agents not to interfere with the movement of other nearby agents. This resulted in problems in goal zones where agents gave up on patterns that were very close to being assembled. When giving up on tasks, the agents should detach blocks and move on with only two blocks. This was not always the case, since agents didn't detach indirectly connected blocks. These agents didn't seem to be aware of the indirectly connected blocks when moving around afterward. They tried to perform move actions that weren't applicable with the indirectly connected blocks.

7.2 GOAL-DTU vs. MLFC

We lost no matches against MLFC. This was also by fortune, as the second match was a 0-0 draw.

MLFC spent a lot of resources clearing our agents, with some, albeit limited, success. They did manage to clear GOAL-DTU agents waiting in the goal zones on more than one occasion, which resulted in the GOAL-DTU agents dropping their tasks. Our agents were not defending themselves as well as we intended. This also explains why MLFC managed several critical clears.

As seen in Fig. 38 and Fig. 48, we solve a substantially higher number of tasks than MLFC in the first and third simulation. But the one task that MLFC solves in the third simulation has a very high reward.

In both the second and the third simulation we experience some technical issues, although the issues must be described as more severe in the second simulation. To our luck, MLFC experience equally severe issues in the second simulation, and we manage to get a draw. MLFC is therefore the only team we did not lose a match against (Figs. 35, 36, 37, 39, 40, 41, 42, 43, 44, 45, 46, 47 and 49).

7.3 GOAL-DTU vs. FIT-BUT

FIT-BUT won two of the three simulations. Thus, FIT-BUT is the only team against whom we won just a single match. Clearly, FIT-BUT has developed a strong and effective system, and they manage to submit a very high number of tasks. Even in the first simulation, which we won, FIT-BUT manages to solve more tasks than we do, see Fig. 23. However, the tasks we solve have a higher reward, either due to increased complexity, or because we manage to solve them quite fast (Figs. 20, 21, 22, 24, 25, 26, 27, 28, 29, 30, 31, 32, 33 and 34).

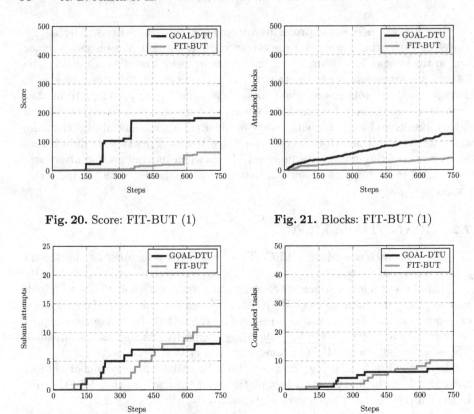

Fig. 20. Score: FIT-BUT (1)   **Fig. 21.** Blocks: FIT-BUT (1)

Fig. 22. Submits: FIT-BUT (1)   **Fig. 23.** Tasks: FIT-BUT (1)

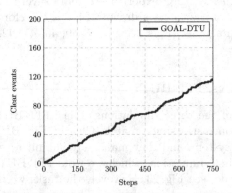

Fig. 24. Clear: FIT-BUT (1)

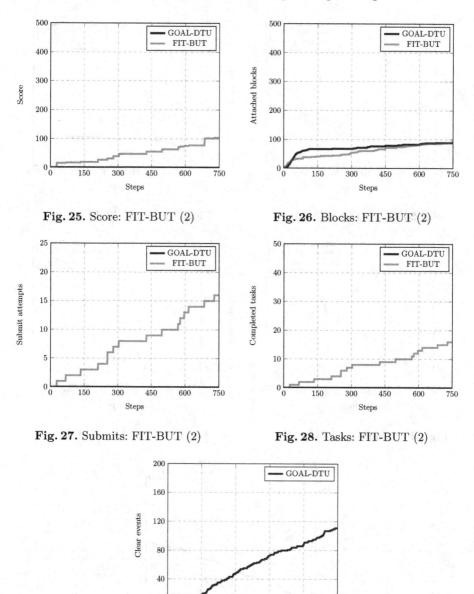

Fig. 25. Score: FIT-BUT (2)

Fig. 26. Blocks: FIT-BUT (2)

Fig. 27. Submits: FIT-BUT (2)

Fig. 28. Tasks: FIT-BUT (2)

Fig. 29. Clear: FIT-BUT (2)

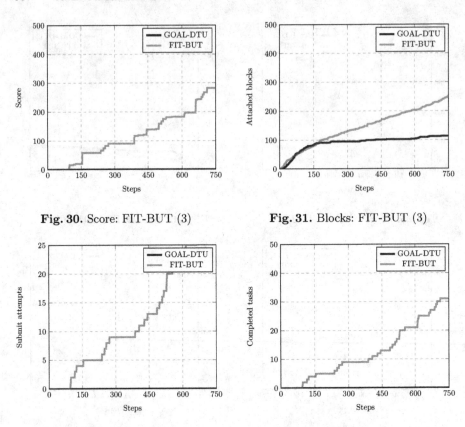

Fig. 30. Score: FIT-BUT (3)   **Fig. 31.** Blocks: FIT-BUT (3)

Fig. 32. Submits: FIT-BUT (3)   **Fig. 33.** Tasks: FIT-BUT (3)

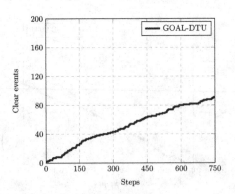

Fig. 34. Clear: FIT-BUT (3)

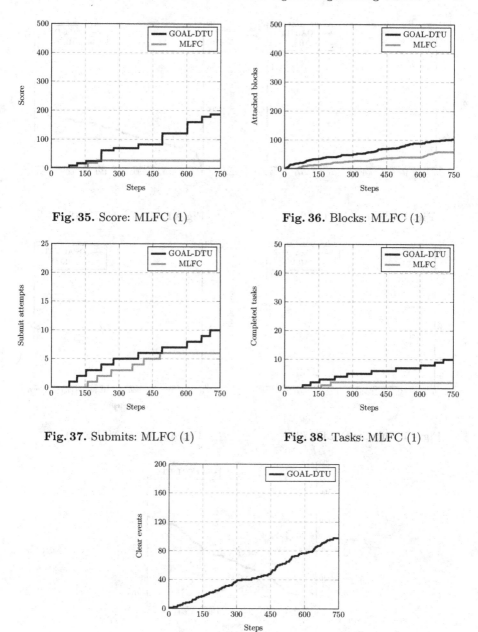

Fig. 35. Score: MLFC (1)

Fig. 36. Blocks: MLFC (1)

Fig. 37. Submits: MLFC (1)

Fig. 38. Tasks: MLFC (1)

Fig. 39. Clear: MLFC (1)

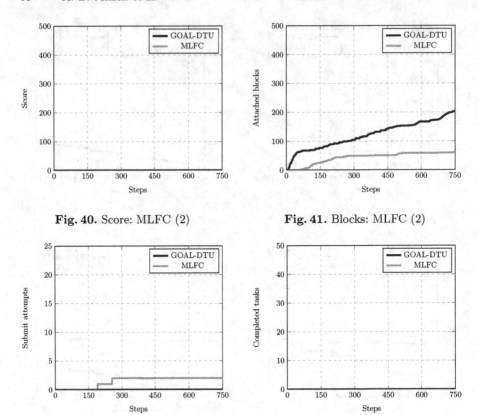

Fig. 40. Score: MLFC (2)   **Fig. 41.** Blocks: MLFC (2)

Fig. 42. Submits: MLFC (2)   **Fig. 43.** Tasks: MLFC (2)

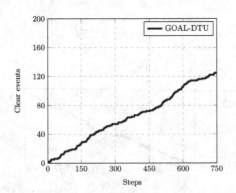

Fig. 44. Clear: MLFC (2)

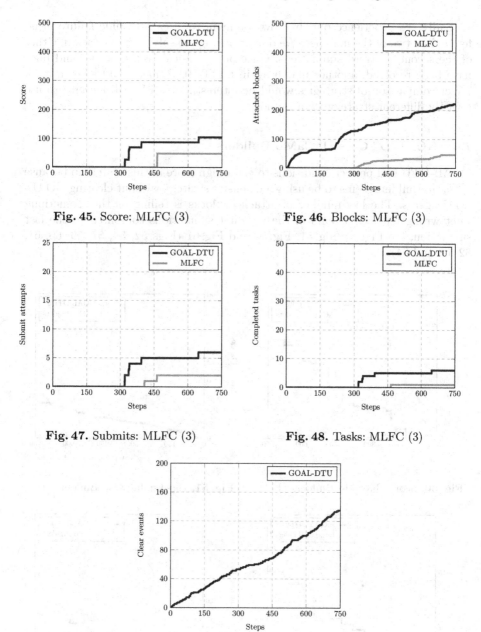

Fig. 45. Score: MLFC (3)   **Fig. 46.** Blocks: MLFC (3)

Fig. 47. Submits: MLFC (3)   **Fig. 48.** Tasks: MLFC (3)

Fig. 49. Clear: MLFC (3)

Sadly, we experience our, by now common, total catastrophic failure in no fewer than two of the matches. We do not manage to solve a single task in either of the second or third simulations. Once our technical issues, errors, and bugs have been resolved, another match against FIT-BUT that would allow a more direct comparison of strategies would be interesting, as FIT-BUT seems to use a vastly different strategy than we do.

7.4 GOAL-DTU vs. JaCaMo Builders

GOAL-DTU had perfect conditions to get a high score in this match up because JaCaMo Builders seems to be using a defensive strategy without clearing GOAL-DTU agents. The low number of attached blocks is telling us that something went wrong for their agents in the two first simulations compared to the last simulation, see Figures Fig. 51, Fig. 56 and Fig. 61 (Figs. 52, 54, 57, 59, 60, 61, 62, 63 and 64).

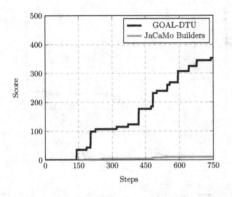

Fig. 50. Score: JaCaMo Builders (1)

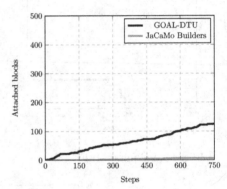

Fig. 51. Blocks: JaCaMo Builders (1)

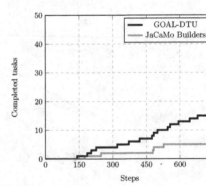

Fig. 52. Submits: JaCaMo Builders (1)

Fig. 53. Tasks: JaCaMo Builders (1)

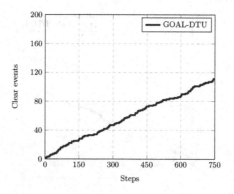

Fig. 54. Clear: JaCaMo Builders (1)

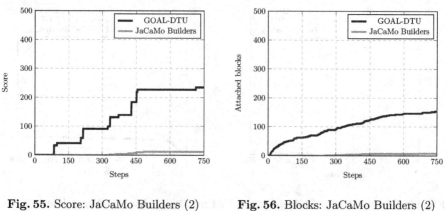

Fig. 55. Score: JaCaMo Builders (2)   **Fig. 56.** Blocks: JaCaMo Builders (2)

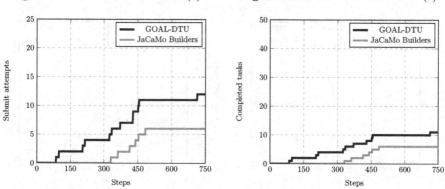

Fig. 57. Submits: JaCaMo Builders (2)   **Fig. 58.** Tasks: JaCaMo Builders (2)

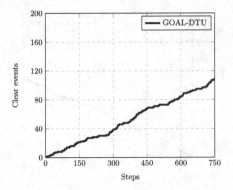

Fig. 59. Clear: JaCaMo Builders (2)

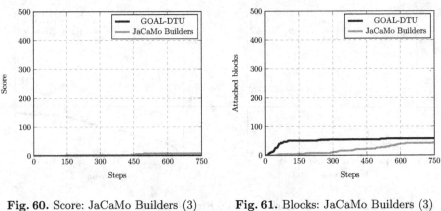

Fig. 60. Score: JaCaMo Builders (3)   **Fig. 61.** Blocks: JaCaMo Builders (3)

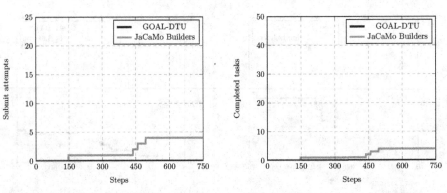

Fig. 62. Submits: JaCaMo Builders (3)   **Fig. 63.** Tasks: JaCaMo Builders (3)

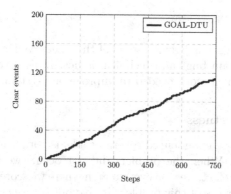

Fig. 64. Clear: JaCaMo Builders (3)

GOAL-DTU's prioritization of tasks combined with the A* path finding algorithm and static plans for tasks resulted in the highest score reached in the contest for all teams. Static plans work well in this case because agents of JaCaMo Builders didn't use much space in the goal zones and didn't clear GOAL-DTU agents in the goal zones.

GOAL-DTU received 22 points on average for the completed tasks in the first simulation, and 21 points on average in the second simulation, see Figures Fig. 50, Fig. 53, Fig. 55, Fig. 58. From step 456 until the end of the second simulation, GOAL-DTU only completes one task, see Fig. 58. It seems like the agents are out of sync and have wrong beliefs about the environment. This continues into the third simulation.

7.5   Free for All

GOAL-DTU is not well suited for simulations with many agents, especially not when the other agents are offensive and use clear actions. GOAL-DTU agents tried to defend themselves with clear actions while waiting in goal zones. The problem is that one agent can only defend against one other agent. If two agents are attacking the same GOAL-DTU agent, its only tactic for dodging clear actions is to move. It won't move due to the use of a static plan. This results in the agent being caught in the opposing agents' clear actions.

The victory in the first simulation seems a bit lucky. GOAL-DTU agents were attacked multiple times by agents from a second team while standing in goal zones. Agents from a third team appear before the attackers succeed. They try to clear the attackers such that the attackers have to move. The GOAL-DTU agents use this opening to submit the tasks.

These openings were less present in the second simulation with thirty agents. FIT-BUT assembles their patterns outside the goal zones such that agents are constantly moving. It's very hard to clear a moving agent, and FIT-BUT used that well to defend themselves.

8   Discussion

The following section sheds light on some of the issues we faced, both regarding system design, program bugs and technical issues. Lastly, we consider some of the further development work needed to improve our system.

8.1   System Robustness

During the contest, we experienced severe problems concerning robustness due to false information. When the problem did not occur, we generally achieved competitive scores. In fact, we won every match where we scored points. However, we identified occurrences of this problem in five out of twelve matches.

False information is detrimental to our system. The current version relies heavily on information being correct which is also the reason for our extensive connection-protocol between agents. The assumption that all agent offsets are correct allows the system to determine the dimensions of the map from the discrepancies of the agent offsets (as touched upon in Sect. 3). If an agent somehow incorrectly updates its location, this can lead to agents agreeing on incorrect dimensions of the map. In this case, no coordinates in the belief base will reflect their actual positions, and as a result the agents will be rendered useless. While this suggests that the system is not robust enough, one could also argue that, once false information is introduced into the system, we cannot expect coherent behaviour.

8.2   Technical Issues

We now shed light on some of the technical issues we faced when deploying our agent system.

Following the competition, we found a bug in the `eismassim` interface implementation. The bug caused agents to sometimes desynchronize with the server, ultimately hampering our agents' performance significantly. The root of the problem lies in the `eismassim` interface which connects the GOAL program to the server running the simulation: when the `eismassim` interface receives a step update from the server while still serving an agent response from the last step, the response will wrongfully be marked as responding to this updated step, and `eismassim` will then block the agent until the next request from the server. As a result, the `eismassim` interface will forward an outdated response to the server, and the agent is responding to a step *before* the agent has received the corresponding percepts from the server. In some cases, this synchronization error caused discrepancies between the believed location of the agent and its actual location, eventually leading the agents to infer the wrong map dimensions. Once an agent is stuck in this out-of-sync state, it cannot recover by itself.

We experienced a connection problem in cases where an agent was located on top of a task board or dispenser. While the agent would recognize this object, other agents would not perceive the object on which the agent was standing. This would potentially lead to non-matching connection requests, and in the worst case, wrongful connections. Ultimately, this would eventually paralyze the system and require a complete reboot.

8.3 Further Work

The technical issues regarding server synchronization and the rare connection problem have been fixed since the competition. However, there is still some general bug fixing left before the system works as intended. In particular, our implementation of a strategy using clearing was not working as intended during the competition and needs some attention. We consider it a prerequisite for more advanced improvements to fix most of these bugs.

We saw in the free-for-all simulations that our agents have a hard time assembling the patterns in the goal zone when a lot of other agents are present. This is due to the quite static approach our system takes when assembling tasks. An obvious improvement would be to give agents the freedom to change the point of assembly, without losing too much efficiency. This might allow the agents to assemble the pattern outside goal zones, and then simply have the submit agent move into the goal zone afterward.

Another observation we have made during the contest is that, especially in larger maps with lots of agents, we have too many idle agents. Once the map is explored and an agent has connected two blocks, the agent will simply roam the map waiting to be assigned a task. We have ideas that could lead to the idle agents being put to better use—for example by protecting goal zones.

Our system could be improved to better utilize a goal-driven approach, with a proper goal-hierarchy. For now, our agents only rely on very high-level goals, and the more intricate details are represented as beliefs. We intend to improve on this aspect in the future where agents have more hierarchical goals, i.e. high-level goals contain a number of sub-goals.

9   Conclusion

We have covered the main strategy of our agents. It is primarily based around proactive (and reactive) collection of blocks while exploring the map. Our agents reactively compose plans to solve available tasks that describe how patterns are to be aligned. While solving tasks, our agents will react to obstacles they meet along their way. When feasible, the agents employ the A* path finding algorithm to optimize short-term movement.

We have described how our agents acquire knowledge from the map, mainly as a result of an initial exploration strategy. We have further described how our agents communicate and utilize this knowledge to move around the map and complete tasks.

We have evaluated the performance of our system during the contest and have found that the system performs well for maps with few agents. As the number of agents increase, the system increasingly fails to assign all agents to tasks, and the assigned agents are less able to maneuver and assemble patterns inside the goal zones.

Finally, we have discussed ideas for general improvements to the system alongside a number of encountered issues. This includes both issues related to the system implementation but also regarding server connections.

In conclusion, we are satisfied with our placement for the contest and with the improvements we have made to the system compared to last year.

Acknowledgments. We thank Tobias Ahlbrecht, Asta Halkjær From and Benjamin Simon Stenbjerg Jepsen for discussions.

A   Team Overview: Short Answers

A.1   Participants and Their Background

What was your motivation to participate in the contest? To work on implementing a multi-agent system capable of competing in a realistic, albeit simulated, scenario.

What is the history of your group? (course project, thesis, ...) The name of our team is GOAL-DTU. We participated in the contest in 2009 and 2010 as the Jason-DTU team, in 2011 and 2012 as the Python-DTU team, in 2013 and 2014 as the GOAL-DTU team, in 2015/2016 as the Python-DTU team, in 2017 and 2018 as the Jason-DTU team and in 2019 as the GOAL-DTU team. We are affiliated with the Algorithms, Logic and Graphs section at DTU Compute, Department of Applied Mathematics and Computer Science, Technical University of Denmark (DTU). DTU Compute is located in the greater Copenhagen area. The main contact is associate professor Jørgen Villadsen, email: 'jovi@dtu.dk'

What is your field of research? Which work therein is related? We are responsible for the Artificial Intelligence and Algorithms study line of the MSc in Computer Science and Engineering programme.

A.2   Statistics

Did you start your agent team from scratch or did you build on your own or someone else's agents (e.g. from last year)? We used as starting point our code from the MAPC 2019.

How much time did you invest in the contest (for programming, organizing your group, other)? We used approximately 160 h to qualify. From January until the contest we used approximately 300 h.

How was the time (roughly) distributed over the months before the contest? To qualify we used approximately 80 h in August and 80 h in September. In January we updated GOAL—the new version of GOAL was not compatible with most of the old code, thus a lot had to be rewritten. We also had to spend some time debugging GOAL itself. In February, the actual programming of the agents started.

How many lines of code did you produce for your final agent team? 2000 lines of code.

How many people were involved? 5 people: Jørgen Villadsen, Alexander Birch Jensen, Benjamin Simon Stenbjerg Jepsen, Erik Kristian Gylling and Jonas Weile.

When did you start working on your agents? We started working on our code from MAPC 2019 in August. As mentioned in the previous questions, large parts of the existing code had to be rewritten, however. This began in January.

A.3 Technology and Techniques

Did you make use of agent technology/AOSE methods or tools? What were your experiences?

Agent programming languages and/or frameworks? We used GOAL. We find that it is very intuitive and relatively easy for newcomers to learn which is an advantage as the programming team changes.

Methodologies (e.g. Prometheus)? No.

Notation (e.g. Agent UML)? No.

Coordination mechanisms (e.g. protocols, games, ...)? No.

Other (methods/concepts/tools)? We used the Eclipse IDE for programming (it has a GOAL add-on).

A.4 Agent System Details

How do your agents decide what to do? The agents reactively decide on their actions based on the current percepts, their beliefs and their goals.

How do your agents decide how to do it? By predetermined rules and actions.

How does the team work together? (i.e. coordination, information sharing, ...) How decentralised is your approach? The team communicates via messages and channels to share information and agree on plans. The approach is mostly decentralized, but certain planning tasks are currently delegated to a single agent at a time.

Do your agents make use of the following features: Planning, Learning, Organisations, Norms? If so, please elaborate briefly. The agents use planning to choose the tasks to pursue. A single agent is chosen to do the planning, but this agent relies on input from all other agents, and the planning agent is chosen dynamically at run time. The planning agent will search through assignment combinations and choose the most promising.

Can your agents change their general behavior during run time? If so, what triggers the changes? An agent will change its behaviour when it is chosen to take part in solving a task.

Did you have to make changes to the team (e.g. fix critical bugs) during the contest? We chose not to make changes during the contest.

How did you go about debugging your system? What kinds of measures could improve your debugging experience? We used log files to record the agents belief base and percepts. We experimented with linear temporal logic, but ultimately it did not make it to the final version.

During the contest you were not allowed to watch the matches. How did you understand what your team of agents was doing? By logging to the console. Admittedly, we could have done much more to improve this aspect.

Did you invest time in making your agents more robust/fault-tolerant? How? We spent some time on this, but not enough. This was one of our problems at the competition.

A.5   Scenario and Strategy

What is the main strategy of your agent team? First, to explore, have our agents find other agents, deduce the map dimensions and agree on a task planning agent. Once this agent has been found, it will continuously inquire the other agents about their available resources and try to create task plans. The task plan is sent to all agents involved in the plan, and these will try to solve it as efficiently as possible.

Please explain whether you think you came up with a good strategy or you rather enabled your agents to find the best strategy. We defined the strategy for our agents. Obviously, the agents have to find strategies for solving tasks and some aspects are only loosely defined.

Did you implement any strategy that tries to interfere with your opponents? We worked on some clearing strategies to defend goal cells, but they seemingly did more harm than good at the competition.

How do your agents decide which tasks to complete? Each task is ranked based on a simple heuristic based on the reward and the delivery time. The tasks are then checked based on their ranks in decreasing order, and the agents will try to complete any tasks they deem solvable.

How do your agents coordinate assembling and delivering a structure for a task? The agents create structured plans on how to assemble the structure. The plans are continuously checked to see if they remain feasible.

Which aspect(s) of the scenario did you find particularly challenging? It was a challenge that the map was a torus and also that the environment was dynamic.

A.6   And the Moral of it is ...

What did you learn from participating in the contest? We learned a lot about using GOAL to write multi-agent programs. We were reminded of the care it takes to develop and test in multi-agent environments.

What advice would you give to yourself before the contest/another team wanting to participate in the next? Start early, because unexpected problems will occur. Have a clear testing strategy.

What are the strong and weak points of your team? The coordination between agents is working quite well and the A* path finding helps agents to move directly. Agents could be more flexible in helping each other and prioritizing other agents' tasks over their own when it is better for the team.

Where did you benefit from your chosen programming language, methodology, tools, and algorithms? GOAL has built-in functionality that allows agents to communicate with one another and it has a predefined agent-cycle that is suitable for the belief-desire-intention model. A* was used by the agents to determine movement actions for short distances.

Which problems did you encounter because of your chosen technologies? We had problems with the EIS interface. These were most obvious during transitions between simulations. We also had some problems with GOAL and backwards compatibility.

Did you encounter previously unseen problems/bugs during the contest? We had a problem with our agents receiving false information and then not being able to do anything meaningful. This problem was not experienced beforehand—probably due to insufficient testing.

Did playing against other agent teams bring about new insights on your own agents? Yes, our agents are vulnerable to clear actions when they are waiting in the goal zones.

What would you improve (wrt. your agents) if you wanted to participate in the same contest a week from now (or next year)? If the contest was a week from now, we would mainly focus on bug fixing and thorough testing. If we had more time we would make better use of agents when they are not partaking in solving tasks. Also, we might look into some better defensive strategies and continuously revising plans to check if they could be optimized.

Which aspect of your team cost you the most time? We had major problems with a lot of the code not being compatible with the newest version of GOAL. Due to missing unit-tests, the problems were almost impossible to locate, and a lot of code had to be rewritten. This was a major setback. Furthermore, the A* algorithm used more CPU time than expected.

What can be improved regarding the contest/scenario for next year? As has already been suggested, running the agent programs on the server itself. If this was implemented, it would be interesting to decrease the time available for the agents to decide on their actions.

Why did your team perform as it did? Why did the other teams perform better/worse than you did? The A* and coordination between our agents made us fast at completing patterns. However, we had a large setback during January, which meant we had to rewrite most of the additions to the 2019 version, as well as spending some time on GOAL itself. This left little time for debugging. We thus found a lot of bugs during the competition.

If you participated in the "free-for-all" event after the contest, did you learn anything new about your agents from that? We had our suspicions confirmed—that the current strategy will be a lot less effective if there are many agents cluttering the goal zone. For such scenarios, we need a more dynamic task-solving approach.

References

1. Hindriks, K.V., Koeman, V.: The GOAL Agent Programming Language Home (2021). https://goalapl.atlassian.net/wiki
2. Hindriks, K.V., de Boer, F.S., van der Hoek, W., Meyer, J.-J.C.: Agent programming with declarative goals. In: Castelfranchi, C., Lespérance, Y. (eds.) ATAL 2000. LNCS (LNAI), vol. 1986, pp. 228–243. Springer, Heidelberg (2001). https://doi.org/10.1007/3-540-44631-1_16
3. Hindriks, K.V.: Programming rational agents in GOAL. In: El Fallah Seghrouchni, A., Dix, J., Dastani, M., Bordini, R.H. (eds.) Multi-Agent Programming, pp. 119–157. Springer, Boston (2009). https://doi.org/10.1007/978-0-387-89299-3_4
4. Hindriks, K.V., Dix, J.: GOAL: a multi-agent programming language applied to an exploration game. In: Shehory, O., Sturm, A. (eds.) Agent-Oriented Software Engineering, pp. 235–258. Springer, Heidelberg (2014). https://doi.org/10.1007/978-3-642-54432-3_12
5. Boss, N.S., Jensen, A.S., Villadsen, J.: Building multi-agent systems using Jason. Ann. Math. Artif. Intell. **59**, 373–388 (2010)
6. Vester, S., Boss, N.S., Jensen, A.S., Villadsen, J.: Improving multi-agent systems using Jason. Ann. Math. Artif. Intell. **61**, 297–307 (2011)
7. Ettienne, M.B., Vester, S., Villadsen, J.: Implementing a multi-agent system in python with an auction-based agreement approach. In: Dennis, L., Boissier, O., Bordini, R.H. (eds.) ProMAS 2011. LNCS (LNAI), vol. 7217, pp. 185–196. Springer, Heidelberg (2012). https://doi.org/10.1007/978-3-642-31915-0_11

8. Villadsen, J., Jensen, A.S., Ettienne, M.B., Vester, S., Andersen, K.B., Frøsig, A.: Reimplementing a multi-agent system in Python. In: Dastani, M., Hübner, J.F., Logan, B. (eds.) ProMAS 2012. LNCS (LNAI), vol. 7837, pp. 205–216. Springer, Heidelberg (2013). https://doi.org/10.1007/978-3-642-38700-5_13

9. Villadsen, J., et al.: Engineering a multi-agent system in GOAL. In: Cossentino, M., El Fallah Seghrouchni, A., Winikoff, M. (eds.) EMAS 2013. LNCS (LNAI), vol. 8245, pp. 329–338. Springer, Heidelberg (2013). https://doi.org/10.1007/978-3-642-45343-4_18

10. Villadsen, J., From, A.H., Jacobi, S., Larsen, N.N.: Multi-agent programming contest 2016 - the Python-DTU team. Int. J. Agent-Oriented Softw. Eng. **6**(1), 86–100 (2018)

11. Villadsen, J., Fleckenstein, O., Hatteland, H., Larsen, J.B.: Engineering a multi-agent system in Jason and CArtAgO. Ann. Math. Artif. Intell. **84**, 57–74 (2018)

12. Villadsen, J., Bjørn, M.O., From, A.H., Henney, T.S., Larsen, J.B.: Multi-agent programming contest 2018—the Jason-DTU team. In: Ahlbrecht, T., Dix, J., Fiekas, N. (eds.) MAPC 2018. LNCS (LNAI), vol. 11957, pp. 41–71. Springer, Cham (2019). https://doi.org/10.1007/978-3-030-37959-9_3   ·

13. Jensen, A.B., Villadsen, J.: GOAL-DTU: development of distributed intelligence for the multi-agent programming contest. In: Ahlbrecht, T., Dix, J., Fiekas, N., Krausburg, T. (eds.) MAPC 2019. LNCS (LNAI), vol. 12381, pp. 79–105. Springer, Cham (2020). https://doi.org/10.1007/978-3-030-59299-8_4

MLFC: From 10 to 50 Planners in the Multi-Agent Programming Contest

Rafael C. Cardoso[1]([✉]) [ID], Angelo Ferrando[2] [ID], Fabio Papacchini[3] [ID],
Matt Luckcuck[4] [ID], Sven Linker[5] [ID], and Terry R. Payne[3] [ID]

[1] Department of Computer Science, The University of Manchester, Manchester, UK
rafael.cardoso@manchester.ac.uk
[2] Department of Computer Science, Bioengineering, Robotics and Systems
Engineering (DIBRIS), University of Genova, Genova, Italy
angelo.ferrando@unige.it
[3] Department of Computer Science, University of Liverpool, Liverpool, UK
{fabio.papacchini,trp}@liverpool.ac.uk
[4] Department of Computer Science, Maynooth University, Maynooth, Ireland
matt.luckcuck@mu.ie
[5] School of Computing and Communications, Lancaster University in Leipzig,
Leipzig, Germany
s.linker@lancaster.ac.uk

Abstract. In this paper, we describe the strategies used by our team, MLFC, that led us to achieve the 2nd place in the 15th edition of the Multi-Agent Programming Contest. The scenario used in the contest is an extension of the previous edition (14th) "Agents Assemble" wherein two teams of agents move around a 2D grid and compete to assemble complex block structures. We discuss the languages and tools used during the development of our team. Then, we summarise the main strategies that were carried over from our previous participation in the 14th edition and list the limitations (if any) of using these strategies in the latest contest edition. We also developed new strategies that were made specifically for the extended scenario: cartography (determining the size of the map); formal verification of the map merging protocol (to provide assurances that it works when increasing the number of agents); plan cache (efficiently scaling the number of planners); task achievement (forming groups of agents to achieve tasks); and bullies (agents that focus on stopping agents from the opposing team). Finally, we give a brief overview of our performance in the contest and discuss what we believe were our shortcomings.

Keywords: Multi-Agent Programming Contest · Multi-Agent Systems · Automated Planning · Agents Assemble · JaCaMo

Work supported by UK Research and Innovation, and EPSRC Hubs for "Robotics and AI in Hazardous Environments": EP/R026092 (FAIR-SPACE) and EP/R026084 (RAIN). Cardoso's work is also supported by Royal Academy of Engineering under the Chairs in Emerging Technologies scheme.

T. Ahlbrecht et al. (Eds.): MAPC 2021, LNAI 12947, pp. 82–107, 2021.
https://doi.org/10.1007/978-3-030-88549-6_4

1   Introduction

In this paper, we focus on the strategies used by our team, the Manchester and Liverpool Formidable Constructors (MLFC). We provide some context and basic concepts of the scenario and the simulation environment; however, we assume the reader has some prior knowledge about the Multi-Agent Programming Contest (MAPC)[1] in order to better understand our contributions.

The 15th edition of the MAPC[2] is part of an annual competition in the area of multi-agent programming. This latest edition extended the "Agents Assemble" scenario from the 14th MAPC [1]. The main goal of the scenario remained the same: two teams of agents compete in a 2D grid to fulfil tasks that are randomly generated by the simulation server, and those teams that complete tasks successfully receive some currency, with the aim of maximising this currency. These tasks comprise assembling and delivering complex block structures of random size, and possibly requiring blocks of different types. A match starts once both teams have connected to the server, and then it proceeds synchronously with each simulation step having a 4 s timeout for agents to submit their actions for that step. A match has 3 rounds, with each round having a random configuration of the servers parameters (different grids, task size, etc.).

The most notable changes to the latest edition of the MAPC include:

1. A circular (i.e., borderless and continuous) grid map; e.g., in a 50 × 50 grid, if an agent at cell 0,0 (i.e., in the top left corner) moves up, it would arrive in cell 0,49 (i.e., the bottom left corner);
2. An increase in the number of agents for each round: 15, 30, and 50 for rounds 1, 2, and 3 respectively (previously this was 10 for all rounds);
3. The addition of a new type of facility called *taskboards*, such that an agent is required to be near a taskboard to accept a task. The same agent must also submit the completed task to the server (previously tasks did not need to be accepted and any agent could submit the task).

Our team, MLFC[3], achieved second place in the 15th MAPC. A prior incarnation of the team, Liverpool Formidable Constructors (LFC), had participated in the previous edition of the competition and won first place. We therefore recapitulate the main strategies used in that edition that were also useful in the new edition of the contest, although for a more comprehensive explanation we refer the reader to [9], which has a complete description of the approach taken by LFC. The main contribution of this work is in the description of the new strategies that were developed specifically for the 15th MAPC. These strategies include: *cartography* – this tackles extension (1) to make our agents capable of discovering the size of the map (information that is unknown during a match); *verification of map merging* – in order to increase the confidence that our previous strategy for merging map information works well when scaling the number

---

[1] https://multiagentcontest.org/.

[2] https://multiagentcontest.org/2020/.

[3] The source code for MLFC is available and can be downloaded from the following URL: https://github.com/autonomy-and-verification-uol/mapc2020-lfc.

of agents, we performed a formal verification of our protocol (thus addressing extension (2)); *plan cache* – our previous strategy of using automated planners to plan the movement of our agents in the grid had to be adapted to cope with extension (2); *achieving tasks* – small changes were necessary to address extension (3), but a number of more significant modifications were required to make efficiency improvements necessary due to extension (2); and *bullies* – the additional agents from extension (2) allowed us to focus some of them to the task of disrupting the activities of the opposing team.

The remainder of the paper is organised as follows. Section 2 lists the languages, tools, and IDEs used during the development of our team. In Sect. 3 we summarise the main strategies that were imported from our previous participation as team LFC, which is followed by Sect. 4 where we describe the new strategies that tackle the main extensions of the scenario. Section 5 contains a brief account of our performance in the matches, and in Sect. 6 we present the responses to a questionnaire created by the contest organisers. Finally, Sect. 7 concludes the paper with an overview of our participation in the 15th MAPC.

2   Languages and Tools

For our submission to the 15th edition of the MAPC, we used the same set of languages, tools, and IDEs to develop MLFC as when we developed LFC with one exception; an additional tool for formal verification. The agents, environment, and organisation were all developed in the JaCaMo framework for multi-agent oriented programming. The IDE used was Eclipse with the JaCaMo Eclipse plugin, whereas the automated planner used was the Fast Downward (FD) planning system. To facilitate the formal verification of the protocol used for map merging. The Communicating Sequential Processes (CSP) formal language was used to verify the correctness of the protocol used for map merging; this involved using a new tool—the Failures-Divergences Refinement (FDR) model checker.

JaCaMo[4] [3,4] is a framework for developing multi-agent systems based on the multi-agent oriented programming paradigm. Unlike the more traditional agent-based languages and tools, JaCaMo models both the environment and the organisation as first class abstractions at the same level as agents, through the use of three complementary approaches: *Jason*, *CArtAgO* and *Moise*. Jason [5] is the language used to program the agents based in the Belief Desire Intention (BDI) model [6,17,18]; CArtAgO [19] is used to program the environment in the Java programming language through the representation of artifacts; and Moise [14] is used to model the organisation into three different dimensions: structural (roles and groups), functional (goals, missions, and schemes), and normative (norms and obligations). JaCaMo combines these three technologies seamlessly into one integrated framework.

The base structure of our code remained unchanged from our participation as team LFC in the previous edition. Each agent has its own artifact which acts as a client to communicate with the competition server. Additionally, we have a

---

[4] http://jacamo.sourceforge.net/.

team artifact that is used as a blackboard to share specific information with all of the agents in our team. Although we are only using the structural dimension of Moise, we expanded the roles used in MLFC and added automated plans for changing roles without losing track of what the agent was doing in its previous role.

Fast Downward[5] [11,12] is a well known automated planner that is still being used as a base planning system for many teams that participate in the International Planning Competition[6]. The planner takes as input a domain and a problem specification, written in the Planning Domain Definition Language (PDDL) [16], and generates a solution as output. Our representation remains the same as last time: the domain is created at design time and remains static at run-time, whereas the problem is compiled at runtime and includes only those 61 cells that are observable by the agent that invokes the planner.

CSP [13] is a formal language designed for specifying concurrent communicating systems. A CSP specification is built out of *processes*, which describe the sequence of *events* that occur as the system evolves. An event is a communication on a *channel* which may declare typed parameters, such that the events occurring on the channel must be composed of parameters matching the channel's type(s). Processes can be offered in sequence, as a choice, or in parallel. Parallel processes may cooperate on a set of channels; they are said to synchronise on the events on these channels, meaning that the events must occur simultaneously in both processes. This is how CSP processes communicate with each other, but it is important to note that a process that is not in parallel with another may perform events without requiring another process to 'receive' them. We used CSP to model our protocol for merging the map information of our agents.

FDR [10] is a model checker for CSP specifications, which contains various built-in assertions such as deadlock and divergence (livelock) freedom. FDR also includes the Probe tool, which allows the user to step through the available events in the specification. We summarise how we used FDR to formally verify the map merge protocol in Sect. 4.2, and a full description can be found in [15].

3   Main Strategies Taken from the 14th MAPC

In this section we summarise the three main strategies that we previously used as team LFC in the 14th MAPC and that are broadly used (mostly unchanged) in the 15th MAPC. These three main strategies comprise: 1) *agent identification*, for identifying other teammates when they are encountered in the grid; 2) *building a map*, how to mutually build and share map information between the team; and 3) *planning*, using an automated planner to perform optimal planning based on the observable environment of the agent. Other simpler/smaller strategies continue to be used (for example, exploration strategies and their termination conditions); however, they are not relevant to the new strategies discussed in the

---

[5] http://www.fast-downward.org/.
[6] https://www.icaps-conference.org/competitions/.

next section and thus have been omitted here. Full details of all of the strategies used in the 14th MAPC can be found in [9].

3.1   Agent Identification

As agents do not possess information regarding the identity of other agents at the beginning of each round, they first need to identify their teammates in order to cooperate. Thus, as each agent observes another, it can only recognise whether that agent is a member of its own team (i.e., it does not know which agent it is). One of the first challenges each agent faces, therefore, is one of *agent identification*: when an agent meets another member of its team, it has to try to determine exactly which of its teammates the agent is.

Fortunately, the identification process is not influenced by having a circular map; in fact, the agents only require local information to identify the other members of their team. As all of the information used falls within the agent's observable environment, all coordinates used can be relative to the agent. Thus, it does not matter if some of the positions span across the edges of what would normally be a border. This allows us to reuse the same identification process that we previously used in [9]. In the following, we summarise the main aspects and features of this process, and then provide a simple example of agent identification in practice.

At the beginning of a step, each agent perceives its environment, through the receipt of a set of *perceptions* from the server. These perceptions are checked by the agent to recognise if there are any observed unknown entities which could be part of its team. If this is the case, a broadcast message is triggered by the agent to ask all of the other agents in its team to communicate the details of what they can currently observe in their respective local environments during that time step. Each agent that receives such a broadcast message has to reply with a list containing all the *thing* perceptions it has (i.e., the objects seen by the agent). This list of *things* is then used by the agent to understand if some agent that it currently observes is the same as that which sent the reply.

This can be done in two steps. First, by determining if the replying agent observes an unknown entity in some position that would correlate with the requesting agent; in which case, the agents may be looking at each other. To verify this, the second identification step consists of checking if there is also a correlation with all of the other *things* observed by the requesting agent (and their relative positions) with those observed by the responding agent. If this is the case, it means that not only the two agents are seeing each other, but that all of the *things* in their local environment coincide. This allows the agent to conclude the identification of another team member. Note that this process may generate false positives; for example if multiple agents are in the same exact formation (seeing the same objects, etc.). When this happens, the unknown entity is identified with multiple identifiers (i.e., where one of them is the right one, but it is unclear which of these it is); thus, the identification process fails and the agent is not identified. Because of this, the identification process needs to be constantly reapplied in subsequent simulation steps until all agents are identified.

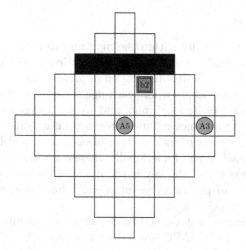

Fig. 1. Identification example with two agents A_5 and A_3, a dispenser of type '$b2$', and black shaded cells representing obstacles.

To better illustrate how the identification process works, we give a simple example (Fig. 1), where we have two agents on the same team: A_5 and A_3. For the sake of simplicity, we focus on the identification process on A_5's side (for A_3 it is symmetric). In this example, we assume that A_5 has not identified A_3 yet, and when the belief thing(4, 0, entity, ''A'') is added to its belief base, it broadcasts an identification request to each agent in its team. When A_3 receives this request, it sends to A_5 the list of things it is currently seeing: [thing(-4, 0, entity, ''A''), thing(-3, -2, dispenser, b2)]. With this information, A_5 first checks whether there is an entity in the list with coordinates (X, Y), and a corresponding entity in its belief base with symmetric coordinates (-X, -Y). In this example, this is satisfied since thing(-4, 0, entity, ''A'') is indeed in the list returned by A_3. Moreover, in A_5's belief base we find thing(4, 0, entity, ''A'') in the corresponding symmetric position. Thus, it is possible that the agent in A_5's local observable environment is in fact A_3. In order to be sure that this is the case, A_5 needs to check that each entity thing(W, Z, Type, Name) in the list, corresponding to the other observed entities in its local environment defined by ($|$W+X$|$ + $|$Z+Y$|$ ≤ 5), is also present in its belief base. This means we can find thing(W+X, Z+Y, Type, Name) in the belief base for each thing in the list (where X and Y are the relative coordinates of A_3 from A_5's viewpoint).

In this example, we have X = 4, Y = 0 and the list containing only one other entity; thing(-3, -2, dispenser, b2). Since $|$-3+4$|$ + $|$-2+0$|$ = $|$ 1 $|$ + $|$ -2 $|$ = 3 ≤ 5, the dispenser should also be in A_5's field of vision, and it is. In fact, we find thing(1, -2, dispenser, b2) in A_5's belief base. Assuming that there are no other teammates at the same distance, A_5 can safely conclude that the agent in its field of vision is A_3. The same process is done by A_3, which will identify A_5 as the agent in its own field of vision.

3.2   Building a Map

In order to move purposefully within the map and to perform tasks efficiently, agents dynamically build a map storing information of the environment that they observe. The map is built following an approach based on the one used in the previous year's scenario [9], where each agent considers its starting position as the $(0,0)$ coordinate of its local map, and stores in this map all the relevant information collected while moving and perceiving entities it observes in its local environment. Thus, the coordinate system of each map will be relative to the starting position of each agent. Functionally, these maps are stored in a CArtAgO artifact as *HashMaps* where the key is the name of the owner of the map and the elements are sets of points representing cells. Furthermore, local maps are merged when meeting other agents.

The main challenges that needed to be addressed in migrating our agents from the 14th to the 15th MAPC are: (1) do the agents need to store more (or conversely less) information regarding entities encountered in the environment, than in the previous year's scenario; and (2) how should the new borderless and continuous map be managed.

The environment consists of a number of entities, some of which are immutable (i.e., the location of the entities remains static throughout a full round), and some of which are dynamic. Whilst some entities are highly dynamic (for example, the agents themselves), other entities can be affected by agent behaviour, such as the movement of a block or the result of a *clear* event[7]. Thus, as the agent moves, it observes its local environment at each time-step, and updates its local map with the location of the following static entities: *dispensers*, *goal positions* and *taskboards*. Whilst there could be utility in retaining information about dynamic entities such as the position of obstacles, blocks and agents, this information may become stale over time and thus is unreliable. Planning (Sect. 3.3) therefore only takes into account knowledge of previously observed static entities, and currently observed entities within the local environment.

Due to the fact that the grid map in this version of the scenario differs from the previous one in that the map is now circular, the map that we store with our previous strategy could appear infinite in scale, with each entity appearing multiple times with different coordinates (i.e., multiples of the actual size of the map itself). Thus there is the risk that an agent may perceive multiple instances of the same entity. To address this problem the cartographers compute and broadcast the size of the map (see Sect. 4.1 for details). Once the information about the size of the map is received by the agents, the maps are normalised accordingly, thus facilitating the easy identification of potential repetitions. The normalisation of the map is not only important to avoid repetitions of elements, but it also allows agents to establish the shortest distance to potential points

---

[7] Clear events occur randomly, but agents have access to a clear action which has a reduced area of effect but otherwise functions the same. A clear event/action will remove any obstacles or blocks and disable any agents that are inside its area of effect.

of interest (e.g., dispenser or goal positions) by going around (of what would normally be) the edges of the map.

The discussion so far has focused on how local maps are built, but the collected information also need to be shared when agents from the same team meet each other. This is when the process of merging maps happens. To start with, all local maps are already stored in the TeamArtifact, meaning that in theory each agent could have access to the other agents' maps. This, however, would not be beneficial if the maps are not merged, as the coordinate system of each agent differs. The full details of the merging process is described in [9], but it is based on the following intuition: suppose that there are two distinct groups of agents G_1 and G_2, where all agents in G_1 have already merged their maps, and likewise, all agents in G_2 have also merged their maps. The map merging process starts when an agent A_1 from G_1 meets an agent A_2 from G_2. The two involved agents, A_1 and A_2, communicate all the relevant information (e.g., their positions and the position of the agent they are seeing) to the respective leaders of the groups; let us call them L_1 and L_2, and the merging process is delegated completely to the leaders. The leaders decide who is going to be the new leader of the group $G_1 \cup G_2$, and merge the information by taking care that no repetition occurs and that all the agents in $G_1 \cup G_2$ share the same coordinate system.

3.3 Planning

As mentioned in the previous section, the dynamic nature of the map and agents moving blocks can make the planning of a route challenging. For this reason, our agents plan their next few actions based on what is observable in their current environment and the static entities stored in the merged map. We use *task planning* as opposed to path planning for the movement of the agents, as we also need to consider other actions (such as the *clear* action) that can alter the way our agents move. Furthermore, since we are dealing with a 2D grid, the problem is simplified as the cells can be modelled as states, and there is no need to use advanced path planning algorithms (due to the fact that we do not have live noisy sensors, nor do we care about collisions).

Planning is not utilised during the initial phase, whereby agents explore the map and compute the map's size. However, once the agents start collaborating with each other, they have sufficient information for planning tasks regarding the existence and location of dispensers, goal positions and taskboards, based on destination information retrieved from the merged maps. The process of reaching the desired destination is an iterative process composed of three stages: 1) selection of a proximal destination that falls within the agents local, observable environment (en route to the actual destination); 2) invocation of the FD planner; and 3) managing the planner's result.

When an agent has a task assigned to it (e.g., heading towards a taskboard or dispenser), it retrieves the global coordinates of the closest cell satisfying its requirements, and translates them into relative coordinates. Then, the agents selects a *good cell* within its observable environment which minimises the overall distance to the actual destination. Such a cell is considered good provided that it does not contain any agent or block (more details on the procedure for the selection of a good cell can be found in [9]). If no good cell can be found, then the agent behaves as if the FD planner has returned an empty plan, which is described later in this section.

Once the agent has selected a good cell, it calls the FD planner via the EISArtifact. In order to invoke the planner, several pieces of information need to be provided: what elements are currently observable by the agent, and how they are represented; what actions are allowed; the goal itself; and whether or not the agent has a block attached to it. First, the details of the agent's observable local environment are already present in the EISArtifact. This allows for the creation of a problem file composed of 61 cells (all the currently observable cells) where the agent is in the centre, dispensers and taskboards are not represented (i.e., they do not constitute obstacles to movements), obstacles are considered obstacles, and blocks and other agents are modelled as blocks. The latter is due to a conservative approach where the planner is not allowed to clear any block, and it is hard to know on-the-fly whether or not the perceived blocks belong to the enemy team (furthermore, this prevents the possibility of us clearing our own blocks by mistake). Second, movement and rotation actions are always permitted, but the clear action is allowed only if the agent has enough energy. From a modelling point of view, allowing or not allowing a clear action is based simply on using a PDDL domain file with or without the definition of the action. Finally, the remaining information (i.e., what the goal is, and whether the agent has a block attached) is provided to the EISArtifact by the agent. Once the EISArtifact has collected all the required information, it produces the problem[8] and domain files used by the FD planner; the planner is then invoked and the results are collected.

Any returned solution (empty or not) is processed by the agent. If a sequence of actions is returned, then the agent blindly executes them in the same order as that within the solution, despite the fact that this can result in some of the actions failing. In this scenario, we adopt a forgiving approach whereby the failure of an action does not necessarily imply that the planner should be called again.[9] The rationale here is that, provided that not all of the actions fail, the agent will still approach the destination, and it reduces the amount of required resources.

The situation is different when the returned plan is empty, or if the agent was unable to locate a good cell in its local environment. In this case, the agent is required to make its own decision regarding its next action. Our approach is for the agent to look for a one-step movement action, which brings the agent closer to its destination, and then to re-invoke the planner. The idea here is that given the dynamic nature of the environment, by making a move towards the

---

[8] An example of a problem file that was generated dynamically during one of the matches can be found at: https://github.com/autonomy-and-verification-uol/mapc2020-lfc/blob/master/planner/example_problem.pddl.

[9] Failures of a movement action are tracked for the agent to have an up-to-date idea of the distance to its destination.

destination, knowledge of the local environment will improve, possibly resulting in the generation of a valid plan. Such a heuristic has so far resulted in good performance of our system, but it is clearly not optimal yet.

It is easy to see how the whole process of planning via the use of the external FD planner does not scale well with an increasing number of agents. To address this issue, our new strategy employs the use of a plan cache, which is described in Sect. 4.3.

4 New Strategies for the 15th MAPC

In this section we describe the details of the main strategies that were developed specifically for the 15th MAPC. These include: *cartography*, to discover the size of the map; *verification of map merging*, to provide assurances about the reliability of the map merging protocol; *plan cache*, to allow up to 50 agents to use the planners efficiently; *bullies*, these are agents that focus solely on disrupting the opposing team by trying to clear their blocks; and *achieving tasks*, to use the new taskboard facility and decentralise task assembly into multiple groups.

4.1 Cartography

One of the main objectives of our implementation is to maintain a map that is common across all of our agents that have identified each other at some point in the simulation. In the 14th MAPC, we were able to identify suitable goal positions and block dispensers by their relative position to the borders of the map. Furthermore, in the initial exploration phase agents randomly chose a direction to explore, and only changed this direction when they approached the border of the map. Since the scenario of this year used a spherical or *circular* map, where the map "wraps-around" on the sides, we can no longer rely on the existence of borders.

Having explored the underlying issues, we realised that the main information we were missing to re-use the previous strategies was the *size* of the map. To obtain the size of the map, we introduced a new role for agents: *cartographers*. The aim of this new role is to find the exact size of the map, in both horizontal and vertical directions (which can be different, for example, we can have grids that are 60 × 50). The size determination occurs in a preliminary phase, before the agents can start with the identification of suitable building sites and assembling blocks for tasks. Cartography is always approached by two agents at once for either horizontal or vertical direction. It is necessary that these two agents have identified each other, and in fact this is what triggers their desire to become cartographers. Only two pairs of cartographers are required; one pair for each dimension (i.e., vertical and horizontal). As soon as two agents adopt the cartographer role for one dimension, they will start to move into opposite directions along that dimension, counting the successful steps they make, until they meet again. For example, if A_1 and A_2 start to work as a pair of cartographers for discovering the size of the horizontal axis, one of them, say A_1 will start to move to the left, while the other, A_2 will move to the right. Since the map folds onto itself, they will necessarily meet again, and can add the number of steps they took to compute the size of the map along that horizontal dimension[10]. This information is then broadcast to all of the other agents in the team.

The cartographers also need to be able to maintain their movement along the axis that they are responsible for exploring. Blocks and obstacles can be cleared by using the clear action. At this stage we do not have to worry about clearing our own blocks, since our other agents are tasked with exploring the grid and will not collect any blocks until the cartography phase has concluded. The only remaining impediment in the path of our cartographers are other agents (friendly and enemy). Friendly exploration agents already avoid other agents they meet on their path by moving around them (e.g., if the are moving south and encounter another agent, they will shift to either east or west, and then continue moving south for a few steps before realigning themselves). We initially planned a similar behaviour for our cartographers in order to avoid enemy agents, tracking the number of cells that the agent moved to ensure that the final calculation remained correct, but due to time constraints this implementation was not finalised in time for the contest. Instead, during the contest if our cartographers were to meet enemy agents along their path that would block their movements, they would simply keep trying to move in the same direction until successful.

Two exploring agents will assume the cartographer role under the following conditions:

- They have just identified each other (as described in Sect. 3.1).
- The size of the map in at least one dimension is unknown by the team.
- There is at least one dimension that has no assigned pair of cartographers that are actively determining its size.

The first condition ensures that the agents can identify each other and thus determine when they meet again having covered the whole length of the map. The other conditions ensure that we have exactly one pair of cartographers for each dimension, while allowing all other agents focus on either exploring the map or disrupting the opposing team (see Sect. 4.4 for the latter). Due to the nature of the maps in the 15th MAPC, agents often start in clusters, which means that the assignment of the four cartographer roles typically occurs during the first step of the simulation.

4.2   Formal Verification of Map Merging

The map merging protocol – which controls how to merge individual agent's maps – was built for the 14th MAPC, and our team reused it for this new edition of the contest. Section 3.2 summarises the protocol, which is described in detail in [9]. In brief, the protocol allows a map used by a group (one or more)

---

[10] When A_1 and A_2 first adopt the role of cartographers, they need to retain the distance between them, as this initial distance has to be added to the final sum.

agents to be merged into another map, pooling the information in both maps and unifying the coordinate system, which enables the group to cooperate. This involves message-passing between several agents (at least 2 and at most 4 per instance of the merge protocol) to coordinate the merge (messages to more agents can be sent after the merge has been completed to update their information).

Having a unified map is critical to the team being able to assemble and deliver tasks, which is why we chose to apply formal verification to the map merging protocol. The protocol had worked well in the 14th MAPC, but testing the protocol was difficult because of the changing environment and interference from the other team in the match.

Verification by Formal Methods encompasses a wide range of mathematically-defined techniques for describing how a system should behave or how it will operate on data, and tools for reasoning about the correctness of these specifications. As mentioned in Sect. 2, we specified the map merging protocol in the formal language CSP and used the model checker FDR for both validation and verification, as described below. A complete description of the specification and verification effort is presented in [15].

The specification was built manually, from careful examination of the agent plans and the description of the protocol in [9]. The specification kept close architectural correspondence with the agent program and protocol: each agent was represented by its own process and given an agent ID, and the agent plans involved in the merge process were represented by events of the same name. This helped with tracing parts of the specification back to their source in the program. The formal specification made some abstractions from the implemented protocol, for example we did not model the agent reasoning cycle. Furthermore, the specification contained three agents; the merge protocol happens between two agents, and the third lets us check that the protocol performs correctly when there is interference.

The protocol specification was also *validated* and *verified*. Borrowing Boehm's descriptions [2], *validation* answers the question "Am I building the right product?" whereas *verification* answers the question "Am I building the product right?". Validating our specification involved checking that it matched the behaviour of the implementation. To verify our specification we checked that it was itself correct and could perform the protocol's behaviour without errors.

Simple validation checks were performed using FDR's Probe tool, which allows a user to step-through the specification. This was invaluable for specification debugging. For more complicated and repeatable checks, we used FDR's built-in [has trace] assertion, which checks that the specification can perform a given trace of events without divergence (livelock), without refusing any of the events in the trace. This assertion was used to check the specification's behaviour in six different scenarios, which were based on the protocol implementation's behaviour during the 14th MAPC. The [has trace] checks were performed automatically by FDR, which made them easy to rerun after updates to the specification (similar to performing regression testing).

For verification of the specification, we checked that it was free from divergence and non-determinism (where the specification may perform several different events, after a given prefix), and that the specification could reach a *done* state—where a *done* event occurs when there is only one map, shared by all the agents. The divergence and non-determinism checks use FDR's built-in assertions, but the *done* check was added to the specification manually. Reaching the *done* state shows that the protocol has behaved correctly and implies that the specification did not deadlock along the way.

We found that CSP was well suited to specifying the map merging protocol, because its features focus on communication and concurrency. FDR provides features that are helpful during specification debugging and verification. The verification effort helped provide additional confidence that the merge protocol worked correctly, and showed how CSP could be applied to Multi-Agent System (MAS) communication protocols. In our previous work we applied CSP to one module of a single autonomous robotic system, as part of a suite of formal verification approaches [7,8]. This verification work shows the utility of applying CSP (and formal verification approaches more generally) to aspects of MAS as well.

4.3   Plan Cache

Using automated planning at runtime is far from being an easy task. The entire process, from encoding the state of the agent as a problem file, to solving it with a planner, is computationally demanding. This can be reasonable for small/simple applications, but can become an issue when applied to large and complex systems, such as a MAS. Indeed, even though the planning problem for a single agent is feasible, it might not be for a coalition of agents where each agent has to perform its own planning as well. Assuming that we had N agents, this would require us to call the planner N times (one per agent). Furthermore, given the MAPC scenario, this could happen for every step of the simulation. Even though individually the problems to be solved are relatively small (remember that we only consider the 61 cells that an agent can observe), calling up to 50 instances of planners (e.g., assuming every agent needs to call the planner in the same step) consumes too many resources. This may not have been a problem if the only thing an agent was required to do in a step was to plan its movement, but in reality there are many operations that every single agent needs to do each step (updating belief base with the dozens of perceptions coming from the server, communicating with other agents, etc.). Of course, more computation power could have also solved (or alleviated) the problem, but we were limited to using laptops (with powerful specifications, but not at the level of high performance computing).

Since physical resources (CPU, memory) and time (how long an agent can wait) are finite, it is always possible to pick a number N of agents for which it is not possible to solve the planning problem in less than a certain amount of time (4 s for each simulation step in the contest). In particular, as we mentioned previously, the 15th edition of the contest extended the scenario to have 15 agents in round 1, 30 agents in round 2, and 50 agents in round 3. Through testing, we noticed that our previous strategy managed to hold up for 15 agents, but it did not work for 30 and 50 agents. Because of this, alternatives to speed up the planning process had to be considered.

We investigated alternatives to speed up the process, and found out that we could make the planning process faster by *caching* the plans. By caching, we refer to the act of storing previously generated plans, instead of simply executing and then forgetting about them. When an agent asks the planner to solve a problem, if such a problem has been already solved in the past, it would be more efficient to retrieve the solution found for this problem, than to generate it again using the planner, resulting in redundant work. This can be achieved by keeping a mapping between *Problem* → *Plan*, which given a problem file, returns its corresponding plan (if present in the cache). When a problem file does not find a match in the cache, it means that it has never been solved before (i.e., a cache miss), in which case the execution continues by calling the planner and then updating the cache. Note that this cache is saved independently of the size of the grid, number of agents, or any other parameter. This means that the cache can be used for any configuration to speed up the planning process.

The first aspect we have to consider for plan caching is how to encode a problem file, so that its retrieval from the cache can be straightforward. Such an encoding must uniquely identify a problem file. Thus, all the information which characterises the agent's local environment needs to be considered.

Given details of an agents local environment, a possible numerical encoding can be obtained by unrolling the grid as a one-dimensional array. This unrolling starts from the upper most cell, and then all rows are appended one by one from left to right. The encoding works as follows: empty spaces are mapped[11] to 0 (dispensers and the agent current position are considered empty), obstacles to 1, blocks to 2, and the movement target (plan goal) to 3. After the contest we realised that since blocks are considered as obstacles for the planner, we could have set their value to 1, which would have decreased the number of cached plans by at least a small margin.

Once the encoding has been created, it can be used to query the cache. Since we want to reuse the cached plans across different executions, the cache is stored in the secondary memory; specifically, each cached plan is stored in a separate file, where the encoding of the agent's local environment is used to name such a file. Consequently, to check if a certain planning problem has already been solved, it is sufficient to check to see if a file exists that is named as the encoding of the problem. If such a file exists, there is no need to call the planner since the corresponding plan is already available within the file; otherwise, the planner is called and a new file is stored (named after the encoding of the problem).

As we have seen previously, it is possible to call the planner in two different settings. The first one corresponds to the generation of a plan by the agent itself; the encoding of which is discussed above. The second occurs when the agent possesses a block (i.e., a block is currently attached to that agent), and requires a plan. The encoding for this is almost identical, except that in this case

---

[11] The mapped values are not semantically relevant, as long as is preserved for all mappings.

we append the local environment coordinates of the block that is attached (note that our planning domain only supports movement with no more than a single attached block). For example, if there is a block attached to the agent and the block is located one cell below the agent, then we would append the string '01' to the beginning of the encoding.

4.4 Bullies

For the 15th MAPC we decided to add attack strategies for our agents. We created a new role for this called *bully*, whereby a bully is an agent with a single and specific purpose: to clear the blocks used by the enemy team. In our solution, two typologies of bullies were used: *bouncer bullies* and *hunter bullies*. One of the disadvantages of the strategies adopted by our team for the 15th MAPC was that time was spent during the initial phase to determine the dimensions of the map, prior to building blocks and achieving tasks, whereas other, faster teams could use this time to complete the tasks, thus gaining an advantage. To counter this, we developed *bouncer bullies*, which had the task of slowing down the enemy team in the initial phase of the match (i.e., until our agents were ready to start building tasks), by disrupting their ability to complete and submit tasks. To achieve this, when a bouncer bully finds a goal position, instead of moving away as normally the explorers would do, it starts patrolling such a goal position and the ones close to it. Every time the bully sees an enemy agent with a block, it tries to clear the block. Since clearing requires three steps, the bully does not always succeed. Nonetheless, by being close to a goal position it puts itself in an advantageous position with respect to any approaching enemy agent; to deliver the task the enemy agent has to approach the bully, which increases the possibility of a clear action succeeding.

Once our agents have finished the initial phase and can commence task building, we no longer require bouncer bullies, as agents with the bouncer bully role could be better employed performing another task, rather than staying at a single goal position. For example, it might be possible that a bully agent selected a goal position which is never used by the enemy team. If that is the case, then the bully agent would just waste time patrolling endlessly a goal position where no blocks would ever be cleared. Because of this, in the remaining steps of each simulation (after the cartography phase has concluded), we need a different kind of bully, the *hunter bully*. These agents behave similarly to the bouncer ones; however a key difference is that they move amongst different goal positions. Specifically, a hunter bully starts patrolling a goal position for a finite number of steps, after which, if no enemy agent with a block was observed, it moves to a different goal position (usually in a different goal cluster). In this way, if the agent initially picked a bad goal position, it will eventually arrive in a good one (i.e., one occupied by the enemy team).

For both bouncer and hunter bullies, the policy to defend a goal position is the same. The agent moves in a circle around the goal position (similar to a shark behaviour). In this way, with respect to staying put, the agent has more possibilities to intercept an enemy agent and clear its blocks.

4.5 Achieving Tasks

Our strategy for assembling block structures and achieving tasks remains similar in principle to our previous participation [9]. Before we explain our strategy, we give a couple of reminders about how the scenario works in regards to tasks: to deliver a task, an agent must be inside a goal cell; it is always the case that block structures must be delivered from the position below the agent, i.e., blocks need to be attached south of the agent for them to be delivered.

The previous strategy included the following agent roles:

- *origin agent*: moves to a unoccupied goal position in the bottom-most cell of a goal cluster;
- *retriever*: goes to a dispenser, obtains one block of a type of block required, and moves to one of the available positions around the origin agent.

Once the exploration phase ends, our agents would form one group consisting of 1 origin agent and 9 retrievers (in the previous edition of the MAPC all three rounds had 10 agents).

Due to the inclusion of *taskboards* in the 15th MAPC, we created a new role called *deliverer*. The deliverer waits next to the closest taskboard in relation to the expected goal position of the origin agent. Once enough agents are in place, an appropriate task will be accepted by the deliverer, and retrievers will start moving towards the origin agent to build the block structure required by the accepted task. At the same time, the deliverer will make its way to the position on top of the origin agent, or if that is not possible then any position around the origin that is not below it. Once the building phase is complete, the origin will detach from the block structure and change places with the deliverer, which will then attach to the block structure and deliver the task and will become the new origin. The first retriever to bring its block to the origin will become the new deliverer and will move to the taskboard. This allows us to speed up the time spent between tasks. The previous origin will then become a retriever and go to fetch a new block from a dispenser. An example of such configuration is shown in Fig. 2.

Finally, to make use of the increase in the number of agents, we divided the team into multiple groups. Since each round varies the number of agents (15, 30, and 50), we calculated the number of groups based on the current size of the team in the round: $GroupSize = RoundSize \div 15$. Thus, for rounds with 15 agents we have one group, for 30 we have two groups, and for 50 we have 3 groups (with 5 remaining agents as leftovers). Since we have the addition of two new roles (deliverer and bullies), we also had to plan how many of these roles would be available within a group. A group of 15 agents (agents can join a group later, and in doing so follow this list of priority) has 1 origin agent, 1 deliverer, 12 retrievers, and 1 bully. In the third round (i.e., 50 agents), the last 5 remaining agents will become bullies that are not affiliated with any group.

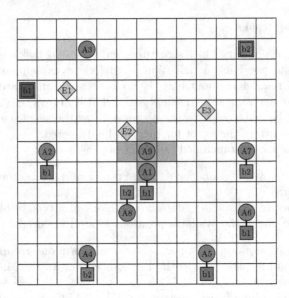

Fig. 2. A 13×13 part of the grid from an execution. Red shaded cells are goal positions, taskboards are cyan shaded cells, blocks of type 'b1' are red squares (dispenser has bold lines), 'b2' blocks are green squares (dispenser has bold lines), enemy agents are green diamonds, and our agents are blue circles. A line between an agent and a block indicates that the block is attached to the agent. (Color figure online)

5   Match Analysis

In this section we provide a brief summary of our performance in the 15th MAPC. We divide our matches into two groups: the first corresponds to the matches played in the first day of the competition, and the second to the matches played in the second day. Each of the five teams had two matches per day.

During the first day, our solution did not perform very well, out of 6 rounds we had 1 win, 1 tie, and 4 losses. This was even more evident in the scenarios with more agents (teams of size 30 and 50, rounds 2 and 3 resp.). The reason for this was due to the computation power required to run the 30 (resp. 50) agents on our machine. Since our solution requires a lot of coordination amongst the agents, when one agent died, it caused a knock-on effect on the other agents, forcing us to restart the whole team. When many agents had to be handled by the machine, sometimes it happened that not all the computations were finished before the deadline (4 s). Specifically, this would happen when a lot of agents were calling the planner, which is the most time demanding component of our solution. As this happened many times during the first day, our solution performed poorly and we lost most of the rounds. For instance, many times our agents were almost ready to start submitting tasks when one of the agents died (lost synchrony with the steps from the server), which caused us to have to restart the whole team. Consequently, restarting the team meant starting from scratch, including doing all of the cartography and exploration again. The overall score obtained by each team in the first day is shown in Table 1.

Table 1. Total score of each team for the first day, with each round being the sum of the two matches that happened in that day. Our team is shown in **bold**.

Team	Round 1	Round 2	Round 3	Total Score
FIT BUT	38	166	188	392
MLFC	**74**	**44**	**66**	**184**
GOAL-DTU	252	100	105	457
LTI-USP	16	34	56	106
JaCaMo Builders	0	18	10	28

During the second day, our solution performed much better, achieving 6 wins out of the 6 rounds, despite the fact that no changes had been made in the code of our solution between the two days. The reason for this improvement in performance is due to the planner's cache. During the first day of the competition, we found that the application did not have enough data from previous matches to build an efficient plan cache; particularly for the two rounds where there were larger numbers of agents (30 and 50 agents respectively), as most of the tests performed prior to the competition were conducted using only 15 agents. Consequently, almost all of the calls to the planner resulted in a cache miss and had to be fully evaluated. Since the planner is the most time demanding component of our solution, by having to compute too many plans, the risk of taking more than 4 s was high (and if this happened, the agent would lag behind and eventually become useless). Because of this, our solution performed poorly in the first day. Nonetheless, we recovered in the second day by having a richer cache of previously computed plans, and our solution outmatched most of the other teams. By having a richer cache, most of the requests for a plan could be satisfied without actually calling the planner. In this way, the computations were lighter, and the risk for an agent to fall behind reduced considerably, which in turn meant we had to restart our team much less often, allowing tasks to be completed successfully (Table 2).

Table 2. Total score of each team for the second day, with each round being the sum of the two matches that happened in that day. Our team is shown in **bold**.

Team	Round 1	Round 2	Round 3	Total Score
FIT BUT	247	252	596	1095
MLFC	**220**	**221**	**383**	**824**
GOAL-DTU	534	235	0	769
LTI-USP	28	48	8	84
JaCaMo Builders	20	22	18	60

Except for the reasons reported above, the performance of our solution has not been influenced greatly by the presence of an enemy team. The only case where our solution had some issues was when the enemy team used agents to clear our blocks. For instance, there was a match where an enemy agent was patrolling a goal cluster and was clearing all the blocks in its local environment. In such scenario, our origin agent failed to build and deliver the tasks because of this. Another peculiar situation happened in a match where an enemy agent was moving around one of our origin agents and managed to steal the block structure that we were building. This happened because at some point our origin agent detaches from the structure to switch places with the deliverer (the agent that accepted the task in the taskboard and thus must be the one to deliver the task). At this exact moment the enemy agent managed to attach to the structure, whereas normally it is not possible to attach to a block if there is any agent from the other team connected to it or to any other block that is connected to the first block.

6   Team Overview: Short Answers

6.1   Participants and Their Background

What was your motivation to participate in the contest?
Three of our members participated in the 14th Multi-Agent Programming Contest as team LFC. We decided to participate in the 15th MAPC because the scenario was the same (with some extensions), so we could use most of our existing code and then focus on improving it.

What is the history of your group? (course project, thesis, ...)
We had three new members for the 15th edition of the contest. Even though at that time most of us were postdoctoral researchers at the University of Liverpool, many of us have changed affiliations since then, but decided to continue to collaborate and participate in the latest MAPC.

What is your field of research? Which work therein is related?
Our members have worked in many different areas of research, but at the moment the intersection of the knowledge in our group relates to formal verification and logical reasoning. Some of our members also have a strong background on agent programming and agent-based tools, while for others they were aware of it but did not have much experience.

6.2   Statistics

Did you start your agent team from scratch or did you build on your own or someone else's agents (e.g. from last year)?
Our code is based on our participation (team LFC) in the 14th MAPC.

How much time did you invest in the contest (for programming, organizing your group, other)?
Approximately 200 h.

How was the time (roughly) distributed over the months before the contest?
Some of the months we were able to dedicate more time to it, but there was a spike in activity in the month before the qualification and then another one in the month before the contest.

How many lines of code did you produce for your final agent team?
A total of 9,805 lines of code, with 3,570 lines in Java (including test files and environment artifacts) and 6,235 lines in Jason agent code.

How many people were involved?
Our team had six members.

When did you start working on your agents?
We started working on April 7th 2020, but implementation was limited to a couple of days during some of the months that followed.

6.3   Technology and Techniques

Did you make use of agent technology/AOSE methods or tools? What were your experiences?

Agent programming languages and/or frameworks?
We used the Eclipse IDE with the JaCaMo plugin. Some of our members were already familiar with it and it has performed very well in past contests.

Methodologies (e.g. Prometheus)?
We did not use any AOSE method.

Notation (e.g. Agent UML)?
We used normal UML sequence diagrams for specifying some of the protocols we created, but without any agent notation. The sequence diagrams were sufficient to specify what we needed.

Coordination mechanisms (e.g. protocols, games, ...)?
Moise (part of JaCaMo) was used for the coordination of agents, especially for task coordination. Some of our communication protocols were implemented ad-hoc just using message passing in Jason (based on the sequence diagrams).

Other (methods/concepts/tools)?
We used the Fast-Downward planner for performing efficient AI task planning. The planner was used off-the-shelf with no modifications required.

6.4   Agent System Details

How do your agents decide what to do?
Our agents evaluate the beliefs coming from the server at any given step, and based on this information they decide what is the best course of action. Their decision can change in the middle of a step from incoming messages of other agents in the team (e.g., requesting for help).

How do your agents decide how to do it?
Most actions are straightforward, but for long distance movement we call an AI task planner that will plan the best route for the agent (it does so iteratively, based on the observations of the agent on the local environment).

How does the team work together? (i.e. coordination, information sharing, ...) How decentralised is your approach?
Relevant team information is shared on a blackboard (CArtAgO team artifact) to save communication time, but for the most part everything is decentralised.

Do your agents make use of the following features: Planning, Learning, Organisations, Norms? If so, please elaborate briefly.
Our agents use an AI task planner for planning their movement for any phase that comes after the exploration phase. A Moise organisation is used to help to coordinate the agents during task assembly and delivery.

Can your agents change their general behavior during runtime? If so, what triggers the changes?
Our agents can be explorers, cartographers, deliverers, task origins, retrievers, and bullies. All agents start as explorers but upon meeting certain conditions they will swap to another role/behaviour.

Did you have to make changes to the team (e.g. fix critical bugs) during the contest?
No, some small changes were attempted to improve the amount of no actions being sent to the server, but they were unsuccessful.

How did you go about debugging your system? What kinds of measures could improve your debugging experience?
Due to the use of several separate tools, debugging the system proved to be quite hard. More time spent in debugging rather than implementing new ideas may provide better results.

During the contest you were not allowed to watch the matches. How did you understand what your team of agents was doing?
We generated some useful logs that could give us an indication of what was happening, however this should be improved in future versions of our team as the logs used were not very intuitive.

Did you invest time in making your agents more robust/fault-tolerant? How?

We have formally verified the protocol we made to merge map information [15]. Other than this we did not invest much time apart from the last few days before the contest when we tried to make the team more fault-tolerant towards task failures.

6.5   Scenario and Strategy

What is the main strategy of your agent team?

Three main new strategies were developed for this edition of the contest: (a) a cartography system that can scout the map and determine the size of the grid; (b) using cached plans that are automatically generated by an AI planner so that our agents can efficiently move through the map; and (c) bully agents that can disrupt the enemy team.

Please explain whether you think you came up with a good strategy or you rather enabled your agents to find the best strategy.

There is a mix of both. For movement the agents find the best strategy, but the strategy for task assembly remained similar to the 14th edition forming groups of agents around a goal cluster, but this time with more groups of agents.

Did you implement any strategy that tries to interfere with your opponents?

Yes, we had a dedicated role (called bully) that would pursue goal clusters that were unoccupied by our team and clear any blocks from the opponents.

How do your agents decide which tasks to complete?

Our agents decide which task to complete based on the available blocks that are positioned around an active goal cluster.

How do your agents coordinate assembling and delivering a structure for a task?

Assembling is coordinated by an agent with the role of task origin which orchestrates and calls the retrievers (agents with blocks) to help it assemble a block structure. Deliverer agents are assigned to a goal cluster and remain next to a taskboard nearby, which upon receiving a signal from the task origin that a task has been selected it will accept the task at the taskboard and move to the origin position to switch places with the origin agent and deliver the task.

Which aspect(s) of the scenario did you find particularly challenging?

Because we were using an external tool for AI task planning, the most challenging aspect was to maintain good computation performance in rounds 2 and 3 (with 30 and 50 agents respectively).

6.6   And the Moral of it is ...

What did you learn from participating in the contest?
Caching the plans was a really interesting solution, but to be effective we should have executed it a lot more times with 30 and 50 agents.

What advice would you give to yourself before the contest/another team wanting to participate in the next?
Debugging and testing the code as much as possible is better than adding new features.

What are the strong and weak points of your team?
The automated task planning component is both the strong and weak point of our team. When we can call the planner and remain inside the deadline for sending an action it works perfectly (e.g., round with 15 agents), but when the necessary plans are not cached some agents do not send their actions on time and that crashes our team (e.g., rounds with 30 and 50 agents).

Where did you benefit from your chosen programming language, methodology, tools, and algorithms?
Coordination was very simple to achieve with Moise, and agent programming in Jason is straightforward if there is some previous knowledge of Belief-Desire-Intention systems. The planner was essential for reducing the reasoning load of the agents.

Which problems did you encounter because of your chosen technologies?
Debugging our system was hard due to the use of multiple languages and tools.

Did you encounter previously unseen problems/bugs during the contest?
Running it locally, even for 30 and 50 agents would work most of the time. During the contest it mostly did not work, and we believe this could have been caused by the extra latency with the communication to the server.

Did playing against other agent teams bring about new insights on your own agents?
Yes, mostly to show us where our bugs were happening. For the most part we tested only with a single team, since testing with two would be very strenuous to the computer running them, and running it remotely was not feasible for long testing sessions.

What would you improve (wrt. your agents) if you wanted to participate in the same contest a week from now (or next year)?
If the number of agents is this high again we would have to extensively test the cache strategy or stop trying to use external tools, since the deadline is too short to make proper use of them.

Which aspect of your team cost you the most time?
Adapting our past strategies to work with a large number of agents.

What can be improved regarding the contest/scenario for next year?
More actions that support interactions between opposing teams would be interesting (either in the next version of this scenario, or in a new scenario).

Why did your team perform as it did? Why did the other teams perform better/worse than you did?
Our team improved in performance on the second day, despite no changes to the code. This happened because we were able to populate the cache of plans with real data from the previous matches.

If you participated in the "free-for-all" event after the contest, did you learn anything new about your agents from that?
The more agents there are in the map the more problems and bugs we find.

7 Conclusion

In this paper we have described the new strategies that we developed to handle the extensions of the "Agents Assemble" scenario in the 15th MAPC. These strategies all contributed to our performance and resulted in our team (MLFC) obtaining 2nd place in the contest. The increase in the number of agents made it particularly hard to adapt our strategies, namely the use of the automated planners, since instead of up to 10 agents calling an instance of the planner (potentially in the same step), now we had to cope with up to 50 agents. The use of a plan cache was a very effective solution for this problem; however, we underestimated how much the cache could differ depending on the parameters of the round (15, 30, and 50 agents). The use of the new 'bully' role contributed a lot to keeping the score of opposing teams in check by delaying and sometimes even annulling their attempts at assembling blocks and delivering tasks.

Most of our tests were with 15 agents, which did not build a sufficient pool of cached plans for rounds with 30 and 50 agents. This was demonstrated by our poor performance in the first day, when many of our agents could not access a cached plan and had to call a new instance of the planner, and thus, overload the processor and subsequently missing its deadline to send an action to the server. A known issue of our base code is that if our agents miss their deadline (i.e., server registers no action), then it is very likely that they will stop responding and will require to be restarted. This in turn is cascaded into another known issue, which is that in order to restart one agent we have to restart the whole team. Therefore, future extensions of our team for this scenario should consider more extensive testing in rounds with 30 and 50 agents to build a better plan cache, add fault tolerance so that agents can recover if they miss their deadline for sending an action, and add a feature that allows individual agents to be reconnected in case they are not able to recover.

References

1. Ahlbrecht, T., Dix, J., Fiekas, N., Krausburg, T.: The multi-agent programming contest: A Résumé. In: Ahlbrecht, T., Dix, J., Fiekas, N., Krausburg, T. (eds.) MAPC 2019. LNCS (LNAI), vol. 12381, pp. 3–27. Springer, Cham (2020). https://doi.org/10.1007/978-3-030-59299-8_1
2. Boehm, B.: Verifying and validating software requirements and design specifications. IEEE Softw. **1**(1), 75–88 (1984). https://doi.org/10/b8ftdf. http://ieeexplore.ieee.org/document/1695100/
3. Boissier, O., Bordini, R., Hubner, J., Ricci, A.: Multi-Agent Oriented Programming: Programming Multi-Agent Systems Using JaCaMo. Intelligent Robotics and Autonomous Agents Series, MIT Press (2020). https://books.google.com.br/books?id=GM_tDwAAQBAJ
4. Boissier, O., Bordini, R.H., Hübner, J.F., Ricci, A., Santi, A.: Multi-agent oriented programming with JaCaMo. Sci. Comput. Program. **78**, 747–761 (2011)
5. Bordini, R.H., Hübner, J.F., Wooldridge, M.: Programming Multi-Agent Systems in AgentSpeak using Jason. Wiley, Hoboken (2007)
6. Bratman, M.E.: Intentions, Plans, and Practical Reason. Harvard University Press, Cambridge (1987)
7. Cardoso, R.C., Dennis, L.A., Farrell, M., Fisher, M., Luckcuck, M.: Towards compositional verification for modular robotic systems. In: Second Workshop on Formal Methods for Autonomous Systems (FMAS 2020), vol. 329, pp. 15–22. Electronic Proceedings in Theoretical Computer Science, December 2020. https://doi.org/10/gj98fx. http://arxiv.org/abs/2012.01648v1
8. Cardoso, R.C., Farrell, M., Luckcuck, M., Ferrando, A., Fisher, M.: Heterogeneous verification of an autonomous curiosity rover. In: Lee, R., Jha, S., Mavridou, A., Giannakopoulou, D. (eds.) NFM 2020. LNCS, vol. 12229, pp. 353–360. Springer, Cham (2020). https://doi.org/10.1007/978-3-030-55754-6_20
9. Cardoso, R.C., Ferrando, A., Papacchini, F.: LFC: combining autonomous agents and automated planning in the multi-agent programming contest. In: Ahlbrecht, T., Dix, J., Fiekas, N., Krausburg, T. (eds.) MAPC 2019. LNCS (LNAI), vol. 12381, pp. 31–58. Springer, Cham (2020). https://doi.org/10.1007/978-3-030-59299-8_2
10. Gibson-Robinson, T., Armstrong, P., Boulgakov, A., Roscoe, A.W.: FDR3 — a modern refinement checker for CSP. In: Ábrahám, E., Havelund, K. (eds.) TACAS 2014. LNCS, vol. 8413, pp. 187–201. Springer, Heidelberg (2014). https://doi.org/10.1007/978-3-642-54862-8_13
11. Helmert, M.: The fast downward planning system. J. Artif. Intell. Res. **26**, 191–246 (2006). https://doi.org/10.1613/jair.1705
12. Helmert, M.: Concise finite-domain representations for PDDL planning tasks. Artif. Intell. **173**(5–6), 503–535 (2009). https://doi.org/10.1016/j.artint.2008.10.013
13. Hoare, C.A.R.: Communicating sequential processes. Comms. ACM **21**(8), 666–677 (1978). https://doi.org/10.1145/359576.359585
14. Hübner, J.F., Sichman, J.S., Boissier, O.: Developing organised multiagent systems using the MOISE+ model: programming issues at the system and agent levels. Int. J. Agent-Orient. Softw. Eng. **1**(3/4), 370–395 (2007)
15. Luckcuck, M., Cardoso, R.C.: Formal verification of a map merging protocol in the multi-agent programming contest. arXiv:2106.04512 [cs], June 2021
16. Mcdermott, D., et al.: PDDL - the planning domain definition language. Technical report TR-98-003, Yale Center for Computational Vision and Control (1998)

17. Rao, A.S., Georgeff, M.: BDI agents: from theory to practice. In: Proceedings of the 1st International Conference on Multi-Agent Systems (ICMAS), San Francisco, USA, pp. 312–319, June 1995

18. Rao, A.S., Georgeff, M.P.: Modeling rational agents within a BDI-architecture. In: Allen, J., Fikes, R., Sandewall, E. (eds.) Proceedings of the 2nd International Conference on Principles of Knowledge Representation and Reasoning, pp. 473–484. Morgan Kaufmann publishers Inc., San Mateo (1991)

19. Ricci, A., Piunti, M., Viroli, M., Omicini, A.: Environment programming in CArtAgO. In: El Fallah Seghrouchni, A., Dix, J., Dastani, M., Bordini, R.H. (eds.) Multi-Agent Programming, pp. 259–288. Springer, Boston (2009). https://doi.org/10.1007/978-0-387-89299-3_8

The LTI-USP Strategy to the 2020/2021 Multi-Agent Programming Contest

Marcio Fernando Stabile Jr.[1]($\boxtimes$) and Jaime S. Sichman[2]

[1] Instituto de Matemática e Estatística, Universidade de São Paulo, São Paulo, Brazil
mstabile@ime.usp.br
[2] Escola Politécnica, Universidade de São Paulo, São Paulo, Brazil
jaime.sichman@usp.br

Abstract. This paper presents the main features and strategies of the LTI-USP which has participated in the 2020/2021 Multi-Agent Programming Contest. The team was developed using Jason programming language, and its main feature is that agents switch between three different behaviors during the game. We discuss the strengths and weaknesses of our team, particularly using data from the matches that we have participated in the Contest.

Keywords: Multi-Agent Programming Contest · Multi-Agent Systems · Jason

1 Introduction

According to [1], the Multi-Agent Programming Contest (MAPC) is an annual event whose initial objective is to provide a platform for comparing and evaluating systems based on computational logic, developed primarily for knowledge representation. This objective is achieved through a contest, where teams of researchers design intelligent *agents* that must act in a given non-trivial scenario. This scenario, which typically changes every two years, runs on a server where two adversarial teams of agents connect both to receive information from the environment in the form of perceptions and to perform actions that transform this environment. This process of receiving perceptions and taking an action is called a *step'*. Each simulation takes place over a specified number of steps, and at the end the team that has achieved most points wins the match.

The LTI-USP has been regularly participating in the MAPC[1], more particularly in 2009 (jointly with UFSC and UFRGS), 2010 [4], 2012, and 2013 [3]. In this 2020/2021 edition, the LTI-USP team obtained the fourth place with one victory and three losses. In this paper, we describe our strategy, our successes, and our mistakes.

---

[1] In 2016, our team has withdrawn.

Supported by CNPq, Brazil, Grant 140448/2016-0.

T. Ahlbrecht et al. (Eds.): MAPC 2021, LNAI 12947, pp. 108–133, 2021.
https://doi.org/10.1007/978-3-030-88549-6_5

This paper is organised as follows. Section 2 contains the contest scenario description, including the differences from the previous contest. We present our team's strategy and the agents behaviors in Sect. 3. In Sect. 4, we detail the contest results, as well as the situations that arised during the matches. Section 6 contains the answers to the questionnaire created by the contest organisers. Finally, we present our conclusions in Sect. 5.

2   The 2020/2021 Scenario: Agents Assemble II

The 2020/2021 edition of MAPC maintains the scenario of MAPC 2019 called Agents Assemble, but adds new elements. In the scenario, agents on a grid must collect blocks from dispensers and assemble them in formats defined by the simulator to earn points.

The simulator consists of a 2D environment with a dimension not informed to the agents. In this environment, intelligent agents can move freely and find *obstacles* that block the passage. As a change in this year's edition, there is no longer an external limit where agents cannot pass. An agent who moves to the edge of the environment circulates to the other side without any indication. This change adds a new layer of complexity to the movement of the agent. If the agent can not perceive the environment's circularity, it can spend all the steps exploring an environment of seemingly infinite size.

In this scenario, agents are responsible for self-organizing. They need to perform tasks that aim to build structures of different shapes and sizes using connected blocks. These tasks can vary from one to four connected blocks. In addition, there are three different types of blocks. Each type of block is available in a specific *dispenser*. Multiple dispensers are present throughout the environment, but each dispenser only provides one kind of block. Tasks also inform how the agents should assemble the blocks. These tasks have a limited number of steps, where if this time passes, the task expires and can no longer be submitted.

Agents can only submit tasks within regions of the map that are called *goals*. An agent must be within one of these areas connected to the correctly assembled blocks and perform a submission action. If the task has not timed out and the opposite team has not submitted it, the team earns points that vary according to the number of blocks needed and the number of steps since the task started.

Another change in this year's contest was the addition of *task boards*. Although they can consult all the available tasks, an agent can only submit a task after accepting it on one of the task boards. To do this, it must move to a task board and perform an action of accepting a task. As each agent can handle just one task at a time, the addition of task boards means that agents need to move around the map to find a new task when necessary. Moreover, an agent cannot submit a task without moving from the task board to the goal.

The challenge is therefore to design teams of agents that must organize themselves to accept the tasks, collect the correct blocks, assemble them, move to the goals and submit these tasks in order to achieve the highest number of points within a limited number of steps[2].

3   System Design

We implemented our team's agents in Jason, that is an open-source interpreter implemented in the Java language for an extended version of the AgentSpeak language, developed by [2]. Jason implements the operational semantics of the language and provides a platform for the development of multi-agent systems. Since it is a platform designed for developing multi-agent systems, many of the capabilities needed by agents are built into the architecture. These capabilities include exchanging messages between agents and converting JSON messages received from the server into perceptions. Using Jason allowed us to focus our development on the agents' behavior instead of technical aspects, such as communication with the server. In addition to these capabilities presented, our team members already had previous experience with Jason. Combining these capabilities with our expertise has allowed us to develop the agents much faster.

In the following sections, we describe the behaviors of the agents and how we implemented them.

3.1   Exploration

Our agents have three possible behaviors, and each agent is always performing one of these behaviors in a particular step. These behaviors are *exploration*, *task achievement*, and *aid*. The agents that are playing these behaviors are called *explorer*, *owner*, and *auxiliary*, respectively.

At the beginning of the simulation, all agents start as explorer agents, as they do not know where they are or where the other agents on the team are; they have a limited vision over a distance of five cells. Agents do not have information either on the locations of task boards, goals, and dispensers, as these have their positions generated at random.

Another interesting detail of this scenario is how the agents perceive the environment. The agents always perceive the surrounding objects with the coordinates relative to the agents' current position. As an example, in Fig. 1, the lighter area around the agent indicates the range of its vision. In this example, this agent perceives the task board at $(-1, 0)$ coordinates (horizontal and vertical) and does not perceive the enemy team's agent, as it is not within its vision range.

As the agents have a restricted view, the agent must remember what it has already found so it can return to points of interest when necessary. As the agent receives perceptions with coordinates related to its current position, we have created a new coordinate system for each agent, called *absolute coordinates*. This coordinate system is different for each agent, as it's origin coordinate $(0, 0)$

---

[2] In the 2020/2021 competition, this limit was 750 steps.

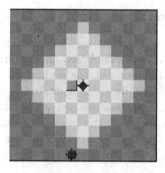

Fig. 1. An agent perceiving a task board.

is the cell in which the agent started the simulation. The agent then stores a belief that symbolizes its current coordinate, and each time it moves, the agent updates this belief.

Thus, we adopted a memory strategy where each agent stores the position of the elements it has already found (dispensers, task boards, goals) according to the distance from its initial position. As an example, suppose that the agent has an absolute position belief $(5, 8)$. This belief indicates that the agent is five cells to the east and eight cells to the south from where it started the simulation. In the case of Fig. 1, this agent receives from the simulator a perception that there is a task board in relative coordinates $(-1, 0)$, that is, one cell to the west of where it is now. This agent then creates a persistent belief that there is a task board at absolute coordinate $(4, 8)$. With that, in the future, it will always be possible to return to this task board.

The agents' exploration strategy then consists of moving around the map recording the perceptions regarding task boards, dispensers, and goals. We decided to store the positions of these three points of interest because they do not move during the simulation. Obstacles, on the other hand, are created and removed randomly during the simulation. Also, there is no reason in our strategy for an agent to move to an obstacle. Therefore, we decided not to store the obstacle positions.

Each agent, when started, randomly chooses a direction (north, south, east, and west). The agent then starts moving in that direction in a straight line and only changes direction in three cases. The first case is when this agent finds something in its path that prevents it from continuing (i.e., another agent or an obstacle). The second case is a random change of direction. At each step, the agent has a 1% chance to change direction randomly. We inserted this behavior to prevent agents from exploring the same place indefinitely since the environment is circular. The third case is when the agent exceeds the exploration limit. As a second way to avoid an infinite exploration of the environment, we define that each agent cannot explore cells that would be more than 100 cells away from its point of origin. In any of the three cases, the agent randomly chooses a new direction and continues to explore.

3.2   Agent Identification

As described in Sect. 3.1, each agent stores information about the environment through an absolute coordinate system based on its point of origin. As each agent starts the simulation in a different cell, the same dispenser will be in a different coordinate for each agent. Despite this, agents need to inform each other the location of the dispensers, task boards, and goals that they have discovered, since this exchange would speed up the process of exploring the environment. To do such a knowledge exchange, we have designed a *mapping system*. In this system, an agent can translate positions to the coordinate system of the other agent.

This task is more difficult because when an agent perceives another agent within his view range, the only information it receives about that agent is to which team it belongs. In other words, an agent has no way of knowing through its perception which one is the other agent that it is perceiving. This identification is needed so that the agent can make the mapping calculations.

To solve both the problem of identifying agents and generating the necessary mapping to transfer knowledge, we developed a strategy for communicating perceptions. Whenever an agent receives a perception informing that it is seeing another agent on the same team, this agent communicates to all other agents that it is perceiving an agent in the respective position and also communicates its current absolute position.

Let us take as an example the situation presented in Fig. 2. In this figure, we can see that *agent*12, which is in the center of the image, receives a perception that there is an agent in the coordinates $(-2, 1)$, that is, two cells to the west and one to the south. As soon as the agent receives this perception, it permanently stores the information that, in the current step, it was in a certain absolute position and noticed an agent in the coordinates $(-2, 1)$. If we assume that this is step number 40 and the agent has an absolute position belief $(5, 8)$, the agent generates a belief entity(-2,1,5,8,40). Likewise, the agent sends a message to all other agents with this information. In our example, all other agents would receive a message entityMessage(agent12, -2,1,5,8,40).

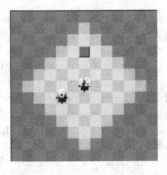

Fig. 2. Two agents recognize each other.

*Agent*6, who in our example perceived and was perceived by *agent*12, performed the same procedure as *agent*12. With this, each agent now has two beliefs related to the agents' position in step 40. One of the beliefs generated by itself and the other was received by a message from the other agent. In the same example, we can assume that *agent*6 has an absolute position belief $(13, -2)$, meaning that *agent*6 is thirteen cells to the east and two cells to the north of its initial position. After exchanging messages, *agent*12 would have the following beliefs in his belief base:

$$\text{entity}(-2, 1, 5, 8, 40)$$

$$\text{entityMessage}(\text{agent}6, 2, -1, 13, -2, 40)$$

Similarly, *agent*6 would have the following beliefs in its belief base:

$$\text{entity}(2, -1, 13, -2, 40)$$

$$\text{entityMessage}(\text{agent}12, -2, 1, 5, 8, 40)$$

Notice that the positions are shifted because *agent*12 perceives *agent*6 two cells to the west and one to the south, while *agent*6 perceives *agent*12 two cells to the east and one to the north. Based on this information, each agent can create a position mapping for the other agent's coordinate system. The agents calculate this mapping through Eq. 1.

$$XMapper = XSenderPos - (XAgPos + XDistance)$$
$$YMapper = YSenderPos - (YAgPos + YDistance)$$

(1)

In our example, for *agent*12, $XSenderPos$ and $YSenderPos$ are the absolute position of *agent*6, whose value is $(13, -2)$. $XAgPos$ and $YAgPos$ are the absolute position of *agent*12, whose value is $(5, 8)$. Lastly, $XDistance$ and $YDistance$ are the relative position of *agent*6 that was perceived, which equals $(-2, 1)$. Applying the formula, we have $XMapper = 10$ and $YMapper = -11$.

After calculating the mapping values, *agent*12 can inform *agent*6 of the position of the task board that it is perceiving. As we can see in Fig. 2, the task board is three cells north of *agent*12. Therefore, it is in the relative position $(0, -3)$. As described in Sect. 3.1, the agent stores the task board position using absolute coordinates. Since in the example, *agent*12 is in the absolute coordinate $(5, 8)$, this task board will be in the coordinate $(5, 5)$. In order to communicate the position of this task board to *agent*6, *agent*12 sends the absolute position $(5, 5)$ and adds the calculated mapping values $(5 + 10, 5 + (-11))$, that is, $(15, -6)$. This calculated value, when received by *agent*6, will correspond to the absolute position of the task board in its coordinate system. One may verify that this calculation is correct by calculating this value for *agent*6. Knowing that the current absolute coordinates of *agent*6 in the example are $(13, -2)$ and that the task board is two cells to the east and four cells to the north $(2, -4)$, we have that the task board coordinate is $(13 + 2, -2 + (-4))$, which corresponds to the value $(15, -6)$ communicated by $agent12$.

It is through this calculation that agents exchange all coordinates. Each time an agent finds a new place of interest, it communicates its position to all agents whose mapping it knows. Similarly, when the agent calculates a new mapping, it sends the coordinates of all points that it knows to the recognized agent.

All these calculations, however, are not useful if the agent is unable to identify which agent it is currently perceiving. In order to be able to identify which agent was perceived, the agent searches among the received messages if any messages are containing the reverse position to which it has perceived. In the example above, $agent12$ perceived an agent at $(-2, 1)$ and received a message from $agent6$ that perceived an agent at $(2, -1)$. A problem that can occur during this identification is that multiple agents may perceive each other in similar positions simultaneously. It is possible, for example, that there are other agents in another area of the environment that are perceiving themselves in the coordinates $(-2, 1)$ and $(2, -1)$. If this happened in our example, $agent12$ would have received two messages with the coordinates $(2, -1)$ and would have no way of knowing which of the two agents it was perceiving. For this reason, the mapping is calculated only if the agent receives exactly one message with the reverse position that it has perceived.

This behavior generates a second problem, which occurs due to the functioning of Jason's architecture. In Jason's architecture, only one message is evaluated per reasoning cycle. Due to the abundance of exchanged messages, the agent can take several reasoning cycles to process messages from all agents. For this reason, after empirical experiments, we defined that a 5-step delay of the simulator would be necessary before starting the mapping process. This delay means that when the agent receives information from the simulator that a new step initiated, the agent analyzes its position and the messages received from other agents referring to five steps before. In our example, the agents perceived and communicated in step 40, but they would only analyze this information and calculate the mapping in step 45 of the simulator.

3.3 Task Owners and Auxiliary Agents

As defined in Sect. 3.1, our agents have three behaviors. All agents start the simulation as explorer agents to find task boards, dispensers, and goals, as described in Sect. 3.1 and to identify other agents and calculate mappings, as defined in Sect. 3.2.

This behavior changes when the agent gets enough information from the environment. At this point, the agent becomes an owner agent. We present the code section responsible for this verification in Algorithm 1. As soon as the agent has in its belief base the positions of at least one dispenser of each type (lines 3, 4, and 5), a task board (line 6), a goal (line 7), and a mapping to at least two free agents (lines 10 and 11), it is eligible to become an owner agent. We fixed, however, a limitation on the maximum number of owner agents, which is one-third of the total number of agents on the team. This limitation serves to have enough auxiliary agents to complete the tasks since owner agents are responsible for coordinating auxiliary agents for the task achievement.

When conditions are true, and the agent executes the plan, it informs the other agents that it is now an owner agent (line 14) and stores that same information in its belief base (line 15). Then, the agent verifies the number of owner agents. If it is greater than one-third of the total number of agents, the agent sends a message to all agents, creating a belief informing them that no other agent can become an owner agent.

During the development, we first tried to count the number of owner agents, similarly to lines 16 and 17, in the preconditions. However, we noticed that this verification was computationally very expensive. As the agents' belief base increased, counting how many agents were owners became more and more costly. As the simulation reached about 200 steps, the agents could not execute any actions anymore before the pre-defined time limit. We then implemented a small change moving the agent verification to the plan (lines 16 and 17) and added a belief the agent could quickly access in line 2. By making this small change, we drastically reduced the agents' response time.

Algorithm 1. Role switching algorithm (from Explorer to Owner).

```
 1:  +!randomWalk :
 2:      not noMoreOwners&
 3:      dispenser(_, _, b0)&
 4:      dispenser(_, _, b1)&
 5:      dispenser(_, _, b2)&
 6:      taskboard(_, _)&
 7:      goal(_, _)&
 8:      .all_names(AllAgents)&
 9:      .length(AllAgents, AgentAmount)&
10:      .count(mapper(AgentName, _, _)&
                 not taskowner(AgentName)&
                 not auxiliar(AgentName, _), AvailableAgents)&
11:      AvailableAgents > 1&
12:      .my_name(MyName)&
13:      not auxiliar(MyName, _)
14:  < −.broadcast(tell, taskowner(MyName));
15:      +taskowner(MyName);
16:      .count(taskowner(Owner), TaskOwnerAmountNew);
17:      if(TaskOwnerAmountNew >= (AgentAmount/3)){
18:          .broadcast(tell, noMoreOwners);
19:          .print("noMoreOwners");
20:      }
21:      !!achieveTask.
```

Once an agent becomes an owner agent, it moves to the nearest task board and accepts a task. We detail the task selection method in Sect. 3.4. Depending on how many blocks are needed to submit the task, the agent executes a different strategy.

In the simplest case, only one block is needed in the task. The owner agent then moves to the nearest dispenser that provides the necessary block, takes the block, moves to the nearest goal area, and tries to submit the task. If the owner agent succeeds, it restarts the process by going to the nearest task board. If this task has already been completed by the opposing team, the agent destroys the block with a clear action and restarts the process.

In cases where more than one block is required in the selected task, the owner agent requests assistance from explorer agents with whom it has a calculated mapping. Once these agents agree to help, they become auxiliary agents. For each additional block, the owner agent asks an agent for help. Therefore, if a task needs two blocks, the owner agent collects one block and an auxiliary agent the other block. In tasks with three blocks, the owner agent asks for help from two auxiliary agents, where each one is responsible for collecting a block.

When the agent owner confirms the agents' assistance, it chooses the nearest goal and calculates the position of the blocks according to the selected task. Aiming to reduce collisions among agents, we defined that owner agents can only occupy the corners of the goal area. We illustrate this concept in Fig. 3, where *agent*26, who is the owner agent, is occupying a cell in the corner of the goal area.

The owner agent, through the use of the mapping, communicates to the auxiliary agents three pieces of information: (i) which block they should collect, (ii) where they should position themselves, and (iii) where they should position the block.

Fig. 3. Two agents preparing the blocks for submission.

At this point, all agents involved in the task (owner and auxiliaries) search for the designated blocks in the nearest dispenser and go to the defined place. When the owner agent positions itself, it sends messages to the auxiliary agents to connect the blocks in the correct order, and once assembled, the owner agent submits the task. Regardless of the success or failure of the task submission, auxiliary agents become explorer agents again and communicate to all agents that they are free to assist in new tasks. In tasks with multiple blocks, the owner agent destroys all the blocks if the task fails. The owner agent then restarts the achieving cycle.

3.4   Task Selection

One of the characteristics of the tasks is the existence of a deadline for their submission. Each task has a step limit, after which it is no longer possible to submit it to earn points. During development, our agents frequently exceeded this limit. The greater the number of needed blocks, the greater the chance of a problem occurring and, consequently, the greater the risk of the agents exceeding the deadline. Also, as the opposing team seeks to achieve the same tasks, the older the task, the greater the chance of the opposing team submitting it. For these reasons, we decided to prioritize tasks based on their creation step and how many blocks are needed. We present the code section responsible for the task selection in Algorithm 2.

We consider "a task of size n" as a task that needs n blocks to be delivered. We found during development that agents were able to submit tasks of size 2 consistently. Tasks of size 3 failed occasionally. On the other hand, tasks of size 4 constantly failed. For this reason, we decided that our agents would not attempt to achieve tasks of size 4, as it would be more beneficial if the four required agents were seeking to accomplish two different tasks of size 2, which would have a much greater chance of success.

When an agent arrives at the task board, it analyzes the task list from the most recently created task. This analysis is possible because task names have a sequential index. The first task created by the simulator is called "task1", the second "task2", and so on. When analyzing the list, the owner agent creates its own list of tasks (Lines 2 to 7). This new list is created by removing from the task list received all the tasks that other owner agents are already trying to achieve (Line 3) and all tasks of size 4 (Line 7). Removing the tasks selected by other agents is important so that there are not multiple agents trying to achieve the same task. The owner agent then searches in the three most recent tasks (with the highest index) for a task of size 2 (Lines 25 to 36). If such a task exists, the most recent task of size 2 is selected (Line 33). In case there are no tasks of size 2 among the three most recent tasks, the agent chooses the most recent task available (Lines 23 and 39). If there are no tasks that the agent can select, the agent waits on the task board until one appears (Lines 8 to 11). Once performed the selection, the owner agent communicates to all other agents the selected task.

We illustrate this concept in Fig. 4. When Agent1 needs to choose a task, it consults the three most recent tasks with a size smaller than 4 that are not selected by other agents. In the example, these would be tasks with names task3, task5, and task6 (task4 is not evaluated due to its size). As one of these tasks has a size of 2 (task3), the agent accepts this task and communicates to the

Algorithm 2. Task selection algorithm.

```
1:  +!getTask
2:  < −.findall(IntTaskNumber, task(TaskName, _, _, TaskRequirements, _)&
3:              not acceptedTask(_, TaskName)&
4:              .delete("task", TaskName, TaskNumber)&
5:              .term2string(IntTaskNumber, TaskNumber)&
6:              .length(TaskRequirements, TaskReqLen)&
7:              TaskReqLen < 4, TaskNameList);
8:      if(.empty(TaskNameList))
9:      {
10:        !performAction(skip);
11:        !getTask;
12:     }
13:     else{
14:        .sort(TaskNameList, SortedTaskNameList);
15:        .reverse(SortedTaskNameList, ReversedTaskNameList);
16:        !getNthTask(0, TaskNameList, SelectedTask);
17:        !performAction(accept(SelectedTask));
18:        .term2string(SelectedTaskTerm, SelectedTask);
19:        !verifyAccepted(SelectedTaskTerm);
20:     }.

21: +!getNthTask(3, TaskNameList, Task)
22: < −.print("Size 2 task not found");
23:      .max(TaskNameList, TaskNumber);
24:      .concat("task", TaskNumber, Task).

25: +!getNthTask(N, TaskNameList, Task)
26:      : .length(TaskNameList, Len)&Len > N
27: < −.nth(N, TaskNameList, TaskNumber);
28:      .concat("task", TaskNumber, TaskName);
29:      .term2string(TaskNameTerm, TaskName);
30:      ?task(TaskNameTerm, _, _, TaskRequirements, _);
31:      if(.length(TaskRequirements, TaskLen)&TaskLen == 2){
32:         .print("Size 2 task found");
33:         Task = TaskName;
34:      }else{
35:         !getNthTask(N + 1, TaskNameList, Task);
36:      }.

37: +!getNthTask(N, TaskNameList, Task)
38: < −.print("Size 2 task not found − insufficient length");
39:      .max(TaskNameList, TaskNumber);
40:      .concat("task", TaskNumber, Task).
```

Fig. 4. Task selection strategy.

other agents that it will try to achieve it. At a later time, Agent2 also needs to choose a task. The agent then consults the three most recent tasks excluding either task4, due to its size, and task3, as there is already an agent working on it. The agent, therefore, evaluates the tasks named task6, task5, and task2. As none of them are size 2, the agent selects the most recent task, which is task6.

3.5   Path Planning

As explained in Sect. 3.3, agents must constantly move to specific locations on the map. If an agent needs to collect a block, it must move to the exact place where the dispenser is. Likewise, an owner agent needs to be within a goal area to submit a task. The efficient movement of agents is a factor of great importance as it increases the chances of successfully submitting a task.

We created two movement strategies. The first strategy is for situations when the agent is not carrying a block and the second for when it is. Having two strategies is necessary because when the agent moves with a block, the agent needs to constantly check if something will prevent the movement of the block and if there is enough space to move.

Moving Without a Block
The agent movement when it does not carry a block is straightforward. The first step is to verify if the agent needs to move horizontally. The agent needs to move when its current coordinate on the horizontal axis is different from the destination's horizontal coordinate. If it is different, the agent moves horizontally until its horizontal coordinate is equal to the destination's horizontal coordinate. An example would be an agent in coordinate $(7, 8)$ that needs to move to the Task Board in coordinate $(14, 6)$. The agent's first step is to move east to coordinate $(14, 8)$. If there are not any obstacles, the agent will execute a sequence of movement actions to the east until reaching the position $(14, 8)$. There are, however, a lot of obstacles, agents, and blocks in the environment that can prevent an agent from moving. For this purpose, we implemented a detour mechanism in the agents, where it diverts from any cells in which it can not pass. This mechanism works by maintaining a memory of which direction the agent wanted to

move. In the previous example, the agent wants to move east from coordinate $(7, 8)$ to the coordinate $(14, 8)$.

We illustrate one of the most troubling movement cases in Fig. 5. In the example, the cells colored in black are obstacles, and as soon as the agent goes through the opening in coordinate $(9, 8)$, it can not simply divert north or south to arrive at its destination. The only way the agent can move east is by returning. In this type of situation, a movement memory is valuable. We can describe our agents' movement strategy through three behaviors:

- **When the agent can not move to the desired direction**, it adds the direction to the Direction Stack and changes its orientation clockwise.
- **When the agent can move to the desired direction, and there is something in the direction stack**, it removes the topmost direction in the Direction Stack and changes orientation to the removed direction.
- **When the agent can move to the desired direction, and the Direction Stack is empty**, the agent moves to the destination.

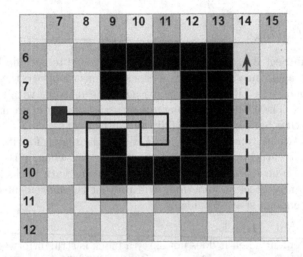

Fig. 5. Movement strategy.

We detailed in Table 1 the steps performed by the agent to complete the deviation shown in Fig. 5. When our agents need to move in a direction and find an obstacle, the agents push to the Direction Stack, a stack data structure, the information on which direction they were following. This behavior is visible in Line 5, Line 7, Line 8, among others. Then the agent tries to move to the next direction clockwise. When the agent manages to move, it removes from the Direction Stack the topmost information and tries to move in that direction again. This behavior is present in Line 6, Line 9, and Line 12, for example. When Direction Stack is empty, and there are no obstacles, the agent moves in the original direction. In this example, direction east. We can see this movement on Lines 1 to 4 and Lines 21 to 26. Notice that the agent did not finish its movement in coordinate $(14, 8)$, as was the initial objective, but in the coordinate $(14, 11)$. This discrepancy, however, is not problematic. As stated earlier, the agent's goal is to reach a cell where its horizontal coordinate is the same as the final destination. Once the agent has arrived, it applies the same method to arrive at the destiny vertical coordinate. In Fig. 5, this movement corresponds to the dashed portion of the path. We do not detail this section of the path as the agent performs it in the same way as the horizontal movement.

Table 1. Agent moving strategy for Fig. 5 scenario.

Line	Coordinate	Verification	Result	Direction Stack	Action	Next Direction
1	(7,8)	move(east)?	true	[]	move(east)	east
2	(8,8)	move(east)?	true	[]	move(east)	east
3	(9,8)	move(east)?	true	[]	move(east)	east
4	(10,8)	move(east)?	true	[]	move(east)	east
5	(11,8)	move(east)?	false	[east]	-	south
6	(11,8)	move(south)?	true	[]	move(south)	east
7	(11,9)	move(east)?	false	[east]	-	south
8	(11,9)	move(south)?	false	[east,south]	-	west
9	(11,9)	move(west)?	true	[east]	move(west)	south
10	(10,9)	move(south)?	false	[east,south]	-	west
11	(10,9)	move(west)?	false	[east,south,west]	-	north
12	(10,8)	move(north)?	true	[east,south]	move(north)	west
13	(10,8)	move(west)?	true	[east]	move(west)	south
14	(9,8)	move(south)?	false	[east,south]	-	west
15	(9,8)	move(west)?	true	[east]	move(west)	south
16	(8, 8)	move(south)?	true	[]	move(south)	east
17	(8,9)	move(east)?	false	[east]	-	south
18	(8,9)	move(south)?	true	[]	move(south)	east
19	(8,10)	move(east)?	false	[east]	-	south
20	(8,10)	move(south)?	true	[]	move(south)	east
21	(8,11)	move(east)?	true	[]	move(east)	east
22	(9,11)	move(east)?	true	[]	move(east)	east
23	(10,11)	move(east)?	true	[]	move(east)	east
24	(11,11)	move(east)?	true	[]	move(east)	east
25	(12,11)	move(east)?	true	[]	move(east)	east
26	(13,11)	move(east)?	true	[]	move(east)	east
27	(14,11)	-	-	[]	-	-

Moving with a Block

When the agent needs to move while carrying a block, the basis of the strategy remains the same. The agent moves first horizontally and then vertically, also using the detour mechanism with the Direction Stack. The difference is in the care that the agent needs to have with the block. When an agent moves, it needs to check if the position for which it will move is free and also if the position for which the block will move is free. Another interesting situation is when the agent needs to move in the same direction as it is holding the block. In cases where the agent is not carrying a block, attempting to move to a cell that contains a block would fail. In cases where the agent moves to the cell where the carried block is, the movement is valid because the block will also move. We had to modify the movement mechanism to take these differences into account.

The first modification aims to allow the agent to know where is the block it is carrying. As soon as an agent connects to a block, it creates a belief that informs it where this block is. If an agent connects to a block in its north, the agent generates the belief carrying(0, -1), for example. This belief is updated when the agent performs a rotation action, to reflect the new orientation of the block.

Having the information of the exact position of the block, we modified the movement behaviors of the agents. We can describe our agents' movement strategy when carrying blocks through four behaviors:

- **When the agent can not move to the desired direction**, it adds the direction to the Direction Stack and changes its orientation clockwise.
- **When the agent can move to the desired direction, but the block can not**, the agent performs a rotation operation to allow the block movement.
- **When both the agent and the block can move to the desired direction, and there is something in the direction stack**, it removes the topmost direction in the Direction Stack and changes orientation to the removed direction.
- **When both the agent and the block can move to the desired direction, and the Direction Stack is empty**, the agent moves to the destination.

The rotation operations of the block are considerably simple when compared to the movement operations. When the block needs a rotation, the agent identifies a direction that is free and rotates clockwise or counterclockwise to position the block in a way that movement becomes possible.

3.6 Achieving Tasks After Unexpected Events

The scenario proposed by MAPC is competitive and highly dynamic. For these reasons, one of the most prominent difficulties is to ensure that the agents can perform the defined strategies as planned. During the development of the agents, we perceived some recurring situations that led to failures in the task submission process, and we implemented modifications to correct problems when they emerged.

The simulator randomly creates what is called a "clear event." These events mark a random-sized area on the map and perform a "clear action" on it. This action disables all agents in the area, erases all blocks in it, and changes obstacles locations in the area and its surroundings. This event is particularly problematic when an agent carries a block to a goal area, and the event erases this block. Another similar situation is that of an opposing agent that uses an action to erase the block carried by the agent. To troubleshoot this kind of problem, an agent that moves with a block constantly checks if it still exists. This verification uses the perceptual information on the block and the belief described in Sect. 3.5 that informs the agent where the block is. If the agent has the belief but does not perceive the block, it was erased. In this case, the agent interrupts its movement and moves toward the dispenser to get a new block.

As described in Sect. 3.3, the owner agent chooses the cell where it will meet the auxiliary agents the moment it selects a task. Due to the highly dynamic nature of the environment, there is no way to ensure that the agents will be able to assemble the blocks in the selected place. Two problems can result in this type of situation. The first is when the cell that the agent chose is not available. The second problem is when there is not enough space to set up the structure of the task. For this reason, the owner agent performs these two checks when it arrives sufficiently close to the cell (to the point of receiving its perceptions). If the agent notices one of these situations, it seeks another unoccupied cell as close as possible and communicates to the auxiliary agents the new coordinates.

As agents only perform the mapping calculation described in Sect. 3.2 when they meet, there may be two owner agents that have no mappings among them. In this case, an agent cannot inform the other where it will assemble the blocks as it does not know the coordinate system of the other. This lack of communication can cause two agents to select the same cell to assemble their blocks. With the behavior described above, the owner agents can solve this situation. However, while this situation happens, auxiliary agents may end up disturbing and causing a task to take longer to complete. Consider an example where agents *agent*1 and *agent*3 are owner agents and agents *agent*2 and *agent*4 are auxiliary agents. In this example, *agent*2 is assisting *agent*1, and *agent*4 is assisting *agent*3. As agents *agent*1 and *agent*3 did not recognize each other, they can not exchange information. Both *agent*1 and *agent*3 choose the same cell to set up the structure of their tasks. The four agents seek the required blocks and head to the appointed place. If *agent*1 arrives first and verifies that the conditions of the space are correct, it then waits for *agent*2 to arrive. The following agent to arrive at the place is *agent*4, which assumes its position designated by *agent*3. When *agent*2 arrives, it can not connect its block to *agent*1 because *agent*4 is in the cell that *agent*2 should occupy. The agents stay in a deadlock until *agent*3 verifies that the cell is occupied and communicates a new location to *agent*4. As unlikely as this situation may seem, it happened several times during the development of the agents of our team. To avoid circumstances like this, we defined that auxiliary agents should wait for the owner agent before positioning themselves. After collecting the block in the dispenser, the auxiliary agents move to the position assigned by the owner agent. However, when they arrive at a cell that is at a five cell distance from their destiny, they stop. Auxiliary agents only approach the designated cell after receiving a message from the owner agent informing that it is positioned and ready to assemble.

4   Match Analysis

Five teams competed in the 2020/2021 edition of the Multi-Agent Programming Contest: FIT BUT, GOAL-DTU, MLFC, LTI-USP, and Jacamo Builders. This edition's winning team was FIT BUT, with ten victories. Our strategy gave us three victories and nine defeats, which yielded the fourth placement.

We present the final score of each team in Table 2. In the contest, each team disputed one match against every other team. Each match is composed of three simulations. In simulation 1, each team uses 15 agents. In simulation 2, each team has 30 agents, and in simulation 3, each team has 50 agents. Each simulation happens in an environment where the agents of the two teams attempt to simultaneously complete the tasks generated by the simulator to earn points. At the end of 750 steps, the team that gained more points wins the simulation. A victory in a simulation awarded three points, and a tie awarded one point.

Table 2. Total score of each team.

Placement	Team	Score
1	FIT BUT	30
2	GOAL-DTU	22
2	MLFC	22
4	LTI-USP	9
5	JaCaMo Builders	6

In this section, we examine the very different strategies proposed by each team. Also, we describe the problems our agents presented during the contest and the results of our matches.

4.1   LTI-USP vs. GOAL-DTU

GOAL-DTU agents use a strategy where as soon as the agent sees a dispenser, it picks up two blocks from it and starts to carry them. When agents decide to achieve a task, they release unnecessary blocks and move the required blocks to a goal area. While moving, one of the agents passes through the task board and accepts the task. This strategy causes the agents to deliver some tasks very quickly, depending on the location of the agents. An example of this was a task submitted in Simulation 2 that yielded 52 points, more than half of the total obtained in any simulation. One similarity between team strategies is that as well as our agents, GOAL-DTU agents do not try to ride structures that need four blocks.

An interesting situation happened in Simulation 1, where our agents were able to submit five tasks while the GOAL-DTU agents only submitted four. Because the GOAL-DTU agents always carry two blocks, they often needed only two agents to complete tasks of size 3. This difference allowed their agents to complete big-sized tasks faster than our agents, earning them more points while completing fewer tasks.

An atypical situation took place in Simulation 3, where GOAL-DTU agents did not accept any task. As a result, our agents completed more tasks which reflected in increasing the score of our team.

At some point in the three simulations, our agents froze. This freezing is something that had not happened during development and took us by surprise. We had to restart the agents, and this ended up damaging their performance. The agents had to repeat the entire exploration procedure, losing many steps from the simulation. Also, some agents stood with blocks attached to them after the restart. Since we haven't prepared the agents for this scenario, they tried to follow the strategy as if the block did not exist. The attached blocks made the agents have many problems moving and completing tasks.

We show the number of points obtained by the teams in each of the simulations in Table 3.

Table 3. Results of the match vs GOAL-DTU.

Team	Sim 1	Sim 2	Sim 3
LTI-USP	16	14	**38**
GOAL-DTU	**65**	**100**	0

4.2   LTI-USP vs. JaCaMo Builders

After the freezing problem occurred with the agents in the previous match, we tried to verify what we could do to prevent the situation from repeating. Between matches, we implemented a quick fix so that the agents would release the blocks after restarting. This fix would avoid agents being stuck with blocks, allowing them to move and work on the tasks as expected.

During simulation 1, we realized that the agents were not able to complete the tasks. Since we could not see what was happening to the agents, we took some time to acknowledge there was a problem. Therefore, we made no points in this simulation. We attributed this problem to the recent update in the agents' source code and reversed the changes. In Simulation 2 and Simulation 3, we used the same source code used against GOAL-DTU. We again had the same freezing problems for the agents. However, we managed to make enough points before this happened to secure the two victories.

We could not identify the strategy used by the Jacamo Builders team. During the three simulations, their agents only completed tasks of size 1, which gave them few points. Also, some agents carried four blocks at the same time. This strategy makes it very difficult for the agents to move.

We show the number of points obtained by the teams in each of the simulations in Table 4.

Table 4. Results of the match vs JaCaMo Builders.

Team	Sim 1	Sim 2	Sim 3
LTI-USP	0	**20**	**38**
JaCaMo Builders	**8**	10	10

4.3 LTI-USP vs. FIT BUT

After the match against the team Jacamo Builders, we had almost a whole day before the match against the FIT BUT team. In this period, we tried to identify the cause of the agents' freezing. Unfortunately, we could not find an answer. Therefore, we implemented and extensively tested a method for the agents to destroy the blocks they were carrying after the restart. With this updated code, we started the second day of the contest.

FIT BUT team agents take a block from the first dispenser they find and stay with it. The agents then accept tasks based on the blocks they already possess. That is, an agent will only accept a task whose initial block is the one they are carrying. Already owning the blocks results in an assembly process that is much faster than ours. Another optimization in the FIT BUT agents is that the agents can identify the closest agent possessing the required block. Once identified, the agents move one towards the other and connect the blocks where they meet. Once the structure is complete, the agent moves to the goal area and submits the task.

An interesting feature of the strategy is that multiple agents can try to reach the same task simultaneously. When an agent is trying to complete the task and another agent completes it before, the agents are able to reuse the blocks they already have connected to complete tasks in the future, further increasing the speed with which they submit the tasks.

FIT BUT agents do not select either tasks of size 4, like our agents and GOAL-DTU agents. Because of their high efficiency in the assembly and submission, their agents submitted many tasks before our agents, which made us obtain very few points.

We show the number of points obtained by the teams in each of the simulations in Table 5.

Table 5. Results of the match vs FIT BUT.

Team	Sim 1	Sim 2	Sim 3
LTI-USP	16	10	0
FIT BUT	**185**	**148**	**314**

4.4   LTI-USP vs. MLFC

After an exploration phase, MLFC agents would position an agent in the goal area and multiple agents around it with a block each. This agent in the goal area receives the blocks from the agents around it and assembles the task. While the other agents assemble the task, the first agent to deliver a block to the agent in the goal area moves to the task board and accepts the corresponding task. This agent then returns, receives the assembled blocks, and submits the task.

MLFC agents were the only ones to assemble and submit tasks of size 4. This possibility provided them many points since none of the other teams would deliver a task of this size before them. Also, always having the blocks positioned near the goal area made the assembly much quicker, yielding more points. A disadvantage of this strategy is that the agents could work on only a few tasks in parallel. In Simulation 1, only one agent positioned itself in the goal area, which resulted in the assemble of only one task at a time. The team had many agents that were only waiting, which wasted part of the team's potential.

Our team was not able to compete with the speed with which they assembled tasks. However, since the agents only did few tasks simultaneously, our agents could assemble and deliver the other tasks in which MLFC agents were not working.

We show the number of points obtained by the teams in each of the simulations in Table 6.

Table 6. Results of the match vs MLFC.

Team	Sim 1	Sim 2	Sim 3
LTI-USP	16	38	8
MLFC	**160**	**195**	**235**

5   Conclusion

In this paper, we have described the strategies used by our team (LTI-USP) in the 2020/2021 MAPC. We employed Jason agents to collect, assemble, and submit the contest's tasks. Our agents create an individual map based on their point of origin and use a mapping system to communicate positions to other agents. Some agents, to which we have given the name of owners, are responsible for picking up tasks in the task boards and coordinating with other agents to assemble the task structures and submit them to earn points.

Our strategy made us have three victories, reaching the fourth position. Although we did not have a good performance in the contest, it is gratifying to see that the agents could perform the defined strategy.

The current MAPC scenario is quite complex, and we learned that multiple strategies are possible. We hope to use the obtained experience to conceive even better agents in the next edition. Among the possible strategy changes, we believe that having all the blocks brought by auxiliary agents would decrease the number of steps needed for assembly. This modification could be even more efficient if these agents have already collected the blocks before the task is accepted.

6   Team Overview: Short Answers

6.1   Participants and Their Background

What was your motivation to participate in the contest?
Our motivation was to build a set of agents that acted in a sufficiently complex environment to validate the results of other researches carried out by the authors in the area of Belief-Desire-Intention architectures.

What is the history of your group? (course project, thesis, ...)
Marcio F. Stabile Jr. is a candidate for a Ph.D. in Computer Science at the University of São Paulo and Jaime S. Sichman is his advisor.

What is your field of research? Which work therein is related?
Both authors research the area of cognitive agents, in particular, BDI agents. We are currently working on novel ways of executing the BDI reasoning cycle.

6.2   Statistics

Did you start your agent team from scratch or did you build on your own or someone else's agents (e.g. from last year)?
Our group built the agents from scratch. The only section of code that was not implemented by our group was the environment, which was provided by the MAPC organizers.

How much time did you invest in the contest (for programming, organizing your group, other)?
A rough estimate would be 400 h used in the design and programming of the agents.

How was the time (roughly) distributed over the months before the contest?
The development started in September 2020 and was completed in January 2021. The time was evenly divided throughout the period.

How many lines of code did you produce for your final agent team?
The code of the agents who participated in the contest has 1985 lines.

How many people were involved?
Both authors were involved in the design, and Marcio F. Stabile Jr. implemented the agents.

When did you start working on your agents?
The design of the agents began in September 2020.

6.3 Technology and Techniques

Did you make use of agent technology/AOSE methods or tools? What were your experiences?
As we plan to use the agents in our research, we only used the Jason framework to develop it.

Agent programming languages and/or frameworks?
We used the Jason framework for creating and running the agents.

Methodologies (e.g. Prometheus)?
We did not use any agent development methodology present in the literature.

Notation (e.g. Agent UML)?
We did not use any agent notation described in the literature.

Coordination mechanisms (e.g. protocols, games, . . .)?
The agents communicate and coordinate through Jason's message system.

Other (methods/concepts/tools)?
No.

6.4 Agent System Details

How do your agents decide what to do?
The agents decide what to do based on the information they have about the environment, the messages they receive from other agents, and the role they are currently playing.

Explorer agents move randomly in search of new information about dispensers, goals, and task boards and, mainly, seek to recognize the team's agents so that they can work together.

Agents playing the role of owners go to the nearest task board in search of tasks. If the task needs more than one block, it asks for help from auxiliary agents so that each one takes a block from the respective dispenser. The owner agent then goes to a goal area where it waits for the auxiliary agents to assemble the blocks and submit the task.

Finally, auxiliary agents are explorer agents who, as soon as they receive communication from owner agents, go to the nearest dispenser to take the requested block to the owner.

How do your agents decide how to do it?
The agents decide how to complete their tasks according to the information they have about the environment.

Exploiting agents communicate only new information to other agents and move in the same direction until they perceive an obstacle.

When choosing a place to assemble the blocks, owner agents, look for the nearest goal area. If the chosen place is occupied by obstacles or other agents, it searches for another place and communicate to the auxiliary agents. The blocks are assembled in a predetermined manner, depending on the configuration in which the blocks are to be placed.

How does the team work together? (i.e. coordination, information sharing, ...) How decentralised is your approach?

Our approach is fully decentralized. Each agent has its mental map of the environment, and communication is done through messages that use mappings that are constituted by the agents when they recognize each other.

Do your agents make use of the following features: Planning, Learning, Organisations, Norms? If so, please elaborate briefly.

Our agents do not use any of these features.

Can your agents change their general behavior during runtime? If so, what triggers the changes?

The only behavioral changes occur when an explorer agent becomes an owner or auxiliary agent. Explorer agents who are aware of the position of at least one dispenser of each type, a task board, a goal area, and have the mapping of two agents who are not owners become owners. However, there is a limit of owners that is one third of the total number of agents. Once the limit is reached, exploiting agents cannot become owner agents. On the other hand, explorer agents who receive a request for assistance from an owner agent become auxiliary agents for the duration of the assistance. As soon as this is over, they become explorer agents again.

Did you have to make changes to the team (e.g. fix critical bugs) during the contest?

We had to make a change after the first day because the agents were freezing, and when restarting them, the agents who were carrying blocks did not know what to do with them, which hampered their movement.

How did you go about debugging your system? What kinds of measures could improve your debugging experience?

Debugging was a complex task since it is a big challenge to keep agents and the environment in sync when using Jason's debugger. To correct the problems, we had to add a series of prints on the behaviors that presented problems to comprehend what was wrong. Moreover, random events make it even harder to discover the source of some issues.

During the contest you were not allowed to watch the matches. How did you understand what your team of agents was doing?

We put some prints in crucial sections of the code to find out what the agents were doing. As an example, we know when an agent changes from explorer to owner, when it selects a task, and when it submits it.

Did you invest time in making your agents more robust/fault-tolerant? How?

We invested much time making the agent more fault-tolerant. In a rough estimate, about 60% of the written code makes the agent recover from unforeseen events. Whether by avoiding obstacles, changing the region where the blocks will be assembled, or recovering blocks that were randomly destroyed, much of the agents' source code would not be necessary if there were no problems during execution.

6.5   Scenario and Strategy

What is the main strategy of your agent team?
Our main strategy is to get agents to recognize the environment and themselves as quickly as possible. Once an agent has enough information, it starts trying to achieve the tasks by asking for help from other agents it already recognizes. Each agent collects a block in the corresponding dispenser, and they meet in the goal area to assemble the blocks and submit the task.

Please explain whether you think you came up with a good strategy or you rather enabled your agents to find the best strategy.
After watching the matches, we realized that we made both right and wrong decisions. A correct decision was not to have agents that carry multiple blocks simultaneously, as this makes it extremely difficult to move the agent around the map. Among the wrong strategy decisions, our agents would not try to deliver tasks of size four. During our tests, they were very subject to failures, and it was rarely possible to achieve a task of this size. This behavior decision caused that if an opposing team quickly delivered such a task, they would have a number of points that would be almost impossible to match.

Did you implement any strategy that tries to interfere with your opponents?
We did not implement any strategy to harm opposing agents.

How do your agents decide which tasks to complete?
When an owner agent arrives at the task board, it prioritizes the most recently created tasks to minimize the chance of it being submitted by the opposing team. Also, when an owner agent selects a task, it warns the other agents on the team not to select the same task. We thought it would be interesting to prioritize tasks of size two, as they would be completed more quickly. This strategy did not prove effective, as the amount of points obtained in this way was not large enough to have a good performance in the contest.

How do your agents coordinate assembling and delivering a structure for a task?
Assembling and delivering is coordinated by the owner agent. It tells auxiliary agents where it is, where the block should be positioned and when to connect the blocks.

Which aspect(s) of the scenario did you find particularly challenging?
The most prominent difficulty was the fact that agents are not able to identify themselves through perceptions. This problem required more effort than initially planned to solve.

6.6   And the Moral of it is ...

What did you learn from participating in the contest?
One of the most challenging aspects of the scenario is the low amount of information each agent possesses. We had to learn how to get agents to coordinate without information that is generally taken for granted, like having an overview of the environment and identifying who the other agents are.

What advice would you give to yourself before the contest/another team wanting to participate in the next?
Focus on completing big-sized tasks quickly. If your agents can do that, they will probably do well.

What are the strong and weak points of your team?
Our team's strong point is its high fault tolerance. The agents have several ways to recover from the most diverse problems that can happen during the simulations. The agents' weak point is how much time they need to organize themselves once they have decided which task to achieve. Another weak point is not trying to assemble tasks of size four.

Where did you benefit from your chosen programming language, methodology, tools, and algorithms?
Because we chose Jason, we were able to use the simulator interface that was already available. This availability avoided a great deal of work to connect the agents to the simulator. In addition, due to our deep knowledge of the internal mechanisms of the Jason framework, we were able to make some small changes to the agents' code that significantly reduced their processing time.

Which problems did you encounter because of your chosen technologies?
The utmost difficulty we had with Jason was using its debugging tool in conjunction with the simulator.

Did you encounter previously unseen problems/bugs during the contest?
Yes. In some matches our agents entered a state where even though they were running and no error message was displayed, all the agents stopped executing actions. We still could not identify the reason for this problem.

Did playing against other agent teams bring about new insights on your own agents?
Watching the matches against the other teams made us realize that some tiny changes could have generated substantial differences in the scores obtained.

What would you improve (wrt. your agents) if you wanted to participate in the same contest a week from now (or next year)?
Currently, owner agents search for one of the necessary blocks for the task. We believe that having all the blocks brought by auxiliary agents would decrease the number of steps needed for assembly.

Auxiliary agents are currently waiting for a message from the owner agent to begin the process of fetching the block and waiting for it near the goal area region. We would modify the agents to stay positioned with a block even before the owner selects a task.

Which aspect of your team cost you the most time?
The aspect that cost the most time was preparing the agents for the greatest possible number of situations in which the original plans would fail. In our experience, agents are rarely able to submit a task without any setbacks.

What can be improved regarding the contest/scenario for next year?
There is a possibility that a particular map configuration can be advantageous to one of the teams. We think it would be interesting for teams to compete against each other on more than one map.

Why did your team perform as it did? Why did the other teams perform better/worse than you did?
As far as we could tell, the number of steps required for assembling tasks is of utmost importance, and our agents were not sufficiently fast. During the simulations, the winning teams were able to submit a few tasks of size 4 quickly, which earned them an enormous amount of points.

If you participated in the "free-for-all" event after the contest, did you learn anything new about your agents from that?
Unfortunately, we were unable to participate in the "free-for-all" event.

References

1. Ahlbrecht, T., Dix, J., Fiekas, N., Krausburg, T.: The multi-agent programming contest: a résumé. In: Ahlbrecht, T., Dix, J., Fiekas, N., Krausburg, T. (eds.) MAPC 2019. LNCS (LNAI), vol. 12381, pp. 3–27. Springer, Cham (2020). https://doi.org/10.1007/978-3-030-59299-8_1
2. Bordini, R.H., Hübner, J.F., Wooldridge, M.: Programming Multi-Agent Systems in AgentSpeak Using Jason. Wiley Series in Agent Technology, Wiley, Hoboken (2007)
3. Franco, M.R., Sichman, J.S.: Improving the LTI-USP team: a new JaCaMo based MAS for the MAPC 2013. In: Cossentino, M., El Fallah Seghrouchni, A., Winikoff, M. (eds.) EMAS 2013. LNCS (LNAI), vol. 8245, pp. 339–348. Springer, Heidelberg (2013). https://doi.org/10.1007/978-3-642-45343-4_19
4. Gouveia, G.P., Pereira, R.H., Sichman, J.S.: The USP farmers herding team. Ann. Math. Artif. Intell. **61**(4), 369–383 (2011). https://doi.org/10.1007/s10472-011-9238-x

JaCaMo Builders: Team Description for the Multi-agent Programming Contest 2020/21

Cleber J. Amaral[1,3], Vitor Luis Babireski Furio[1], Robson Zagre Junior[1], Timotheus Kampik[4], Maiquel de Brito[1], Maicon R. Zatelli[1(✉)], Tiago L. Schmitz[2], Jomi F. Hübner[1], and Mauri Ferrandin[1]

[1] Federal University of Santa Catarina (UFSC), Florianópolis, Brazil
{maiquel.b,maicon.zatelli,jomi.hubner,mauri.ferrandin}@ufsc.br
[2] Santa Catarina State University (UDESC), Florianópolis, Brazil
tiago.schmitz@udesc.br
[3] Federal Institute of Santa Catarina (IFSC), Florianópolis, Brazil
cleber.amaral@ifsc.edu.br
[4] Umeå University, Umeå, Sweden
tkampik@cs.umu.se

Abstract. This paper describes the JaCaMo Builders team and its participation in the Multi-Agent Programming Contest 2020/21 based on the Agents Assemble II scenario. The paper presents the analysis of the scenario and design of the solution; the software architecture, including the tools used during the development of the team; the main strategies; and the results achieved by the team, with challenges and directions for future editions of the contest.

1 Introduction

The Multi-Agent Programming Contest (MAPC) [11][1] is an annual competition with the main aim to stimulate research in the area of Multi-Agent System (MAS) development and programming. The scenario of the MAPC 2020/21 (15th edition), named "Agents Assemble II", is an extension of the previous scenario and brings new challenges for agents, such as a different number of agents in each match[2], the world grid loops horizontally and vertically, and task rewards decrease over time. This scenario is an attempt to stress some key characteristics of MAS, in particular, cooperation, coordination, and decentralization. Our agent team, named JaCaMo Builders[3], was developed by a group formed by five PhDs, two PhD students, and two undergraduate students from different institutions: Federal University of Santa Catarina (UFSC), Federal Institute of Santa Catarina (IFSC), Santa Catarina State University (UDESC), and Umeå University. There are three main aims for our participation in the contest: (i) improve

---

[1] http://multiagentcontest.org.
[2] For simplicity, we use the term "match" to refer to each single round that our team plays in the contest, including the rounds against the same opponent.
[3] https://github.com/jacamo-lang/mapc2020.

© Springer Nature Switzerland AG 2021
T. Ahlbrecht et al. (Eds.): MAPC 2021, LNAI 12947, pp. 134–157, 2021.
https://doi.org/10.1007/978-3-030-88549-6_6

our MAS developing skills, (ii) evaluate new features developed in the JaCaMo platform, and (iii) evaluate some proposals developed in the context of the some of the members' thesis work.

This paper describes the JaCaMo Builders team solution and the organization of the paper is as follows. Section 2 presents an analysis of the scenario, the organization of our group, and the design of the solution. Section 3 gives an overview of the general software architecture used in our implementation, such as programming languages and communication infrastructure. Section 4 discusses the main aspects of our strategy as well as some statistics observed during the competition and comparison to other teams. Section 5 presents tools we have employed to develop and improve our agents. Finally, the conclusions are presented in Sect. 6, where we include a discussion about challenges that we found out during the contest, results, and suggestions for future contests.

2   System Analysis and Design

In the current scenario, a group of agents is situated in a dynamic world grid that loops horizontally and vertically. In the beginning of each match, agents do not know anything about the world[4] and merely have a limited local vision according to the cell in which they are located in a certain moment. The world contains plenty of obstacles that agents cannot cross. These obstacles are changed randomly by means of a *clear* mechanism, which means that some obstacles may disappear while new ones may appear.

A team of agents scores when it accepts some task, acquires blocks, assembles them into the pattern described in the task, and submits the assembled pattern to accomplish the task. Agents can only get tasks if they are close to special cells of the world, named *task boards*. The blocks are acquired close to other special cells of the world, named *dispensers* and, finally, the assembled patterns must also be submitted when the agent is located in special cells of the world, named *goal zones*. The team only scores if all of these steps are concluded before the deadline of the task.

The organization of our group to develop a team of agents to participate in the contest was as follows. Each member or subgroup of our group was more engaged with a specific part of the development of the team, mostly well separated in different and independent strategies that agents could take. We did not use any software engineering methodology or formal method during the development of our team. Instead, we developed the team based on a prototype-driven approach. With the exception of some common parts of the implementation, each specific strategy was tested independently of the others. This made it easier to divide the development among the members of our group.

The MAS was built considering two main dimensions: the environment (Subsect. 2.1) and the agent (Subsect. 2.2). The environment dimension is responsible for mustering the entities that do not have autonomy, such as tools used by the agents, while the agent dimension is responsible for mustering the entities that have autonomy [6].

---

[4] We refer to *world* as the full scenario, including the parts already discovered by the agents and the parts not yet discovered. We refer to *map* as the part of the world already discovered by the agents.

In our analysis of the scenario, we identified some main requirements for the team: (i) agents should be situated in the same map in order to be able to better collaborate with each other; (ii) agents should be able to identify other agents they are seeing in the map[5]; (iii) agents should explore the map as soon as possible to discover the coordinates of *goal zones*, *task boards*, and *dispensers*; (iv) agents should understand the dimension of the map in order to avoid walking around the map longer distances than they should walk to move from a cell to another cell; (v) agents should be able to walk in the map carrying on at least a block in order to avoid getting stuck somewhere due to the presence of obstacles when they need to bring blocks from one place to another; (vi) agents should be able to compute a path between two different cells in the map considering that the map is dynamic and obstacles may appear and disappear.

2.1   Environment Dimension

The environment includes not only the map of the world, but also whatever other tools agents may have access to, to help them achieve some goal or to share some information with other agents. In particular about our team, we decided to provide some functionalities through specific tools. The first one is a tool that lets the agents interact with the MAPC server, so that they can receive updates and send their actions for every step. The second one is a tool that allows agents to store information about the world, in particular the location of everything they can see and discover (a private map). The third one is a tool that allows agents to share information with other agents, in order to synchronize the information about the world when the agents are already situated in the same known world (a shared map). Finally, the fourth tool is to help to create coalitions by means of auctions.

2.2   Agent Dimension

We have identified some specific roles that agents can play in the contest. Two of these roles are related to two main goals: maximize the total score of the team by submitting tasks, and minimize the total score of the opponent team by preventing the approach of opponent agents to *goal zones* and *task boards*. In order to satisfy the first goal, a group of agents adopts a role named *task-builder*, while to satisfy the second goal, a group of agents adopts a role named *defender*. Another important goal is to discover the world as soon as possible, so that, all the agents have the goal to explore the world in the beginning of each match.

Agents use two channels to share information: messages and a shared *blackboard*. Messages are used by an agent when it needs to share a piece of information or when it wants to ask another agent to perform some task. For example, if an agent wants to meet another agent in a certain cell of the map, it sends a message to that agent with the desired location for the meeting. A *blackboard* is a tool that is used by the agents to store a larger amount of information or to communicate with more agents at the same

---

[5] Some technique must be applied to identify agents since the MAPC server merely informs about the presence of an agent, the team it belongs (and not its identifier), and its coordinates according to the observing agent's limited view.

time. Agents store and update information about the map on the *blackboard*, such as the location of the *dispensers*, *goal zones*, *obstacles*, and *task boards*. Each agent starts in a match, having its private *blackboard* with only the information discovered by itself. Agents then merge this information in a shared *blackboard* as soon as they meet other agents, and they identify themselves.

3 Software Architecture

In the current edition of MAPC, we used the EIS-MASSim [4] to communicate with the contest server as well as the JaCaMo[6] platform [5] to develop the MAS. JaCaMo is a framework for MAS programming that combines three separate technologies, each of them being well-known on its own and developed for a number of years, and allows an MAS developer to implement agents, environments, and organizations as first-class abstractions. JaCaMo is a combination of Jason [7], for programming autonomous agents, CArtAgO [12], for programming environment artifacts, and Moise [9], for programming MAS organizations.

The agents are written in the Jason language and the connection of each agent with the contest server is made by means of a CArtAgO artifact, named EISAccess. Each agent has its own EISAccess instance and this artifact has an operation named action that the agent uses to send an action to the contest server. The perceptions provided by the contest server are converted to observable properties and stored in the artifact, so that an agent can perceive the changes in the environment and update its beliefs. We have not used Moise to specify the organization of the MAS; instead, we set the role of each agent in a .jcm file, where we fully specify the configuration of the MAS such as the names of the agents, initial goals, and beliefs. As we have not used Moise, an agent knows its role due to the .asl file that is attributed to it. For each role we have a different .asl file that contains all the plans, goals and beliefs related to the role. For example, an agent responsible for defending the *goal zones* and *task boards* uses the defender.asl file, while agents responsible to build structures of a single block use the individualist.asl file, and agents responsible to build structures of two blocks use the collectivist.asl. In order to reuse code, common code (plans, goals, beliefs, rules) among different roles are kept in other .asl files and included in each strategy that shares the same code. For example, the agentBase.asl musters a bunch of plans, rules, beliefs, and goals that are common for all roles, such as the exploration strategy, walking in the world, interaction with the artifacts and with the contest server, among others.

The source code of the team has about 5914 lines written in the Jason language for the agents' code, about 947 lines for the implementation of the CArtAgO environment, and about 1258 lines of other Java files, totaling 8119 lines.[7]

4 Strategies, Details and Statistics

In this section, we describe the main strategies of our team (Subsect. 4.1) and the main results that we got against other teams (Subsect. 4.2).

---

[6] http://jacamo.sourceforge.net/.

[7] We did not remove comments in the code before counting the number of lines.

4.1 Team Strategies

We considered four main problems to deal with the proposed scenario: world exploration and data synchronization; routing and walking in the world; accepting, building, and submitting tasks; and defense of the *goal zones* and *task boards*. All these "sub-problems" are important in the scenario of the MAPC 2020. Our team of agents is completely decentralised in the beginning of each match. During the beginning of the match, agents try to build a "common map" which is stored in a CArtAgO artifact, shared among all agents. Synchronization in the exploration phase is important to let all agents see the "same world" and it allows agents to make better and faster decisions. Routing plays an important role for the team, because the scenario is quite dynamic, and investing time to make the agents explore such a scenario may give us a good reward during the competition. Most agent decisions are taken in a non-centralised way, but different agents may collaborate, for example to build some structure together. We considered the acceptance, building and submission of the tasks as the core part of this MAPC scenario, as agents need to decide which tasks they could accept and also how to actually build a structure, because it does not depend on a single agent, but a small group of agents. Finally, as a way to maximize our chances to perform better than other teams, the agents need to defend the *goal zones* with the main aim to avoid that the opponent could submit a structure to accomplish its tasks.

World Exploration. The world exploration aims to cover the largest possible map area in the lowest possible step interval. This requires avoiding going twice through the same point. To this end, the agents walk in the world following a strategy based on the Spanning Tree Covering (STC) algorithm [8][8]. The set of coordinates covered by the vision range of an agent is a *cell*. In the MAPC scenario, this set, considering the agent placed at (x, y) with a vision range of r units, is given by the function $Cell$, defined as $Cell(x, y, r) = \{(x^c, y^c) | (x^c, y^c) \in C \wedge |x^c - x| \leq r \wedge |y^c - y| \leq r\}$, where C is the set of all coordinates. The coordinates (x, y) are the center of the cell. Since an agent maps all the elements inside a cell, it can move straight to a coordinate external to that cell to map new objects. The agent (i) records the coordinates that mark the center of the current cell and (ii) chooses a direction to follow to reach the center of the next cell to be explored. It is given by the function $NextCell(x, y, r, d)$, considering that the agent has vision range r, is placed in the coordinates (x, y), and chooses the direction $d \in \{north, south, east, west\}$:

$$NextCell(x, y, r, d) = \begin{cases} (x, y + r) & \text{if } d = north \\ (x, y - r) & \text{if } d = south \\ (x + r, y) & \text{if } d = east \\ (x - r, y) & \text{if } d = west \end{cases} \quad (1)$$

The agent maps all the objects its vision range reaches while moving between two cells. While moving between cells, the agent builds a representation of a tree. The center of

---

[8] Besides STC strategy, we have implemented a spiral strategy. Comparing these two strategies, in the beginning of the exploration, they perform very similarly in terms of mapped area. However, STC discovering rate increases from around step 100, making STC discover about 70% more than spiral strategy in further steps.

each cell is a vertex. The path between the center of two cells is an edge. The leaves of the tree are cells from which there is no free path to a not visited cell. To avoid going through already explored zones, the agents can simply avoid going through existing edges. Besides, when the agents find a blocked route, they can backtrack in the tree until they find a free path to move forward. Each agent builds its own tree, which is merged with the trees of other agents when they share their maps.

Map Sharing. To facilitate teamwork, the agents share their knowledge of the world with each other. Each agent, at the beginning of each match, has its own map with what the agent is discovering in the world. We call this individual map of each agent "LPS" (Local Positioning System). The agents start exploring the world following the exploration strategy. As soon as two agents meet in the world (i.e., they perceive each other), they need to identify who they are seeing. This is achieved by each agent sharing its current picture of what is being seen in the world and comparing it with the other teammates, however looking at it as a mirror view. Agents only consider identifying other agents if no more than 2 agents are situated in the view range. After identifying each other, the agents share their maps and start building a common map. This is repeated until all agents become situated in the same map. We call this common map shared among all agents "GPS" (Global Positioning System). In addition, as the map loops horizontally and vertically, the agents try to determine the correct size of the map, in order to avoid walking around the map several times to arrive to some nearby place. In order to determine the size of the map, we built the following solution, where two agents must meet each other after giving a lap around the map. By our experiments, the number of steps required to find the size is around 450 in the better cases. This number depends on the team size and the map size.

Routing and Walking on the Environment. Walking in the world is a very important aspect for this scenario, considering that the environment is constantly being updated. The routing strategy is responsible for guiding the agents from an origin cell to a destination cell. In our team, agents use the A* algorithm in order to find a route. In every step of the simulation, it updates the route according to the current map of the agent, which means that in every step the agent will use A* to decide which direction it will take to continue to move from the origin to the destination.

The A* algorithm considers the agent and its attached blocks[9], which may constrain some paths, such as in narrow passages between obstacles[10]. It takes into account only the obstacles in the vision range of the agent. By *obstacles*, we mean all items that are insurmountable by the agents, i.e., black cells, the blocks that are dropped in the map and other agents and their attached blocks. If, for some reason, the agent fails to move towards the chosen direction, it will route a path again in the next step. A possible reason for the failure is that the agent meets another agent or a block attached to an agent, which are other moving entities.

---

[9] Our agents are able to walk carrying a maximum of four blocks (a block attached to each side).

[10] The algorithm only routes paths for the agent and its attached blocks in the current rotation, i.e., it does not try other possible rotations.

Accepting, Building, and Submitting Tasks. The group of agents that adopt the role *task-builder* has two main strategies in order to accept and submit tasks, and for each one there is a kind of agent, respectively named *individualist* and *collectivist*. The agent of kind *individualist* is responsible exclusively to accept, complete and submit tasks of a single block, while the agent of kind *collectivist* is responsible to accept, complete and submit tasks that require a maximum of two blocks. The goal behind such strategies is to do simple tasks effectively. We did not focus on more complex tasks because it demands more time to be completed and more sophisticated collaboration and coordination among the involved agents.

In a match, *individualist* and *collectivist* agents start exploring the world until meeting the requirements of a task, and are chosen to perform the task or to help another agent perform a task. After accomplishing or failing in performing or helping in a task, the agents go back to explore the world.

The strategy adopted by the *individualist* agents is advantageous in the sense that agents do not need to collaborate with other agents in order to complete a task. This strategy consists in checking for new tasks until finding a task the agent can perform in order to participate in an auction. For the auction, the agents estimate the number of steps they will take to walk from the current position to the closest *task board*, then to the closest *dispenser* of the specified block, and then to the closest *goal zone*. The best proposal is the minimal estimation of steps. The first one to answer with the best proposal is the winner, i.e., should perform the task. All other agents dismiss this task. Another auction for the same task would only occur in case the winner fails in performing the task[11].

The strategy adopted by the *collectivist* agents consists of one agent accepting a task (we named this agent as *master*), getting a block, and finding an agent to bring a second block (we named this agent as *helper*). In order to find a *helper* agent, the *master* agent starts an auction informing its map, which block it needs and its current position. The agents that are on the same map and know where to find the specified block estimate the number of steps they will take to bring the block to the *master*. The best proposal is the minimal estimation of steps. The first one to answer with the best proposal is the winner. After finding a *helper* agent, the *master* participates in the auction of the task informing its estimated number of steps to bring the first block, plus the estimation informed by the helper. Similarly, the minimal steps estimation and first to propose is the winner, and other agents dismiss this task. Thus, the *helper* agent is hired, i.e., becomes committed to this part of the task. The two agents then combine a meeting place where they meet and build the structure. The meeting place is usually near the *goal zones*. After meeting and connecting the blocks, the *master* agent then performs rotations in order to match the requirements of the task and then submits the final structure. Just like in the *individualist* strategy, fails may drive to new auctions.

Defense of the Goal Zones. Our defense strategy is conceived according to two main goals. The first one is to minimize the chances that the opponent accepts some task.

---

[11] There are three situations considered fails, which result in a complete reset of the agent: agent is lost (its map does not match with its view), agent did not send an action for a number of times, and agent is performing a task that just expired.

The second one is to minimize the chances that the opponent submits a completed task. Broadly speaking, a *defender* agent can achieve the first goal by means of guarding a *task board* against the approach of an opponent agent, and it can achieve the second goal by means of guarding a *goal zone* against the approach of opponents.

A *defender* agent first explores the world, and when a *dispenser* is discovered, it attaches four blocks to itself (one in each adjacent position)[12]. The next step is to find a *goal zone* or a *task board*. After the *defender* agent finds a *goal zone* or a *task board* still not occupied by another *defender*, it stands in the middle of the *goal zone* or *task board* to guard these areas by not allowing the opponent agents to approach them. For the *goal zones* with big areas, our *defender* agents move inside the *goal zone* according to the direction from where the opponent agents come from.

4.2 Comparison to Other Teams

Our team of agents performed not so good in the contest, which led us to achieve the fifth position in the final classification. In our analysis, we point out below the main issues that we found during and after the contest that caused our result.

The first issue was related to transitions between matches, and this issue was found during the contest. For some reason, which we could not understand well, some agents did not perform the transitions between matches correctly. Some of them became disabled during the new match. In order to solve this problem during the contest, we had to restart the full MAS, and it made all our agents start playing in the new match from scratch, and, as a consequence, losing part of the first steps and having to explore the world again.

The second issue was related to our defense strategy, which did not work well during the contest. The *defender* agents were getting the blocks and going to the *goal zones* or *task boards*, however, they did not perform movements to avoid that the opponent agents approach the areas that they were guarding. In addition, the transition issue was found more problematic in the *defender* agents and because of that, the *defender* agents became disabled during most part of the contest.

Our team of agents lost most matches during the contest; however, among the matches that our team won, one of them was particularly interesting. It was the third match against GOAL-DTU. In this match, our agents behaved like in most of the matches, accomplishing a small amount of tasks. In contrast, agents of GOAL-DTU seemed not to be able to accomplish any task. What we could notice is that our agents were occupying the *goal zones* (red cells) for long times (Fig. 1, where the blue square agents are the GOAL-DTU agents and the green diamond agents are the JaCaMo Builders); *i.e.*, GOAL-DTU agents apparently did not try to approach to the *goal zones*.

---

[12] In our strategies, agents only catch blocks from *dispensers*, ignoring dropped blocks.

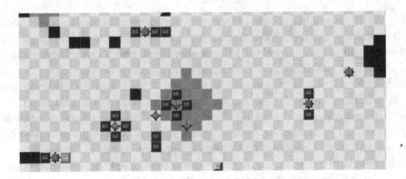

Fig. 1. Screenshot of the match 3 against GOAL-DTU showing our agents (green diamonds) occupying a goal zone (red cells). (Color figure online)

Figure 2 illustrates a situation we have experienced in the first two matches, where our agents, for some reason, did not occupy the *goal zones*. The result against GOAL-DTU made us think that a more robust defense strategy could have made a difference in the contest.

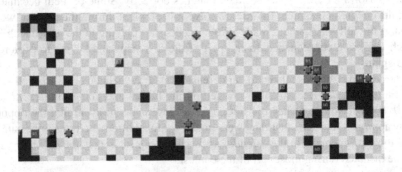

Fig. 2. Screenshot of the match 1 against GOAL-DTU showing that the goal zones (red cells) were not occupied by our agents (green diamonds). (Color figure online)

Another particularly interesting match happened against LTI-USP, and it demonstrated that not always an opponent avoids walking into a *goal zone* occupied by our agents. Figure 3 presents the exact moment when two agents of LTI-USP joined a *goal zone* occupied by one of our *defender* agents, where the green diamond agents are the LTI-USP agents and the blue square agents are the JaCaMo Builders agents.

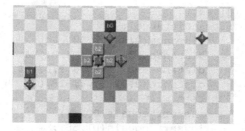

Fig. 3. Screenshot of a match against LTI-USP where our agents (blue squares) occupied a *goal zone* (red cells) but have not avoided that LTI agents (green diamonds) enter the *goal zone*. (Color figure online)

5   Developing and Improving Agents

In this section, we introduce some tools we have used to develop and improve our agents, as follows. Subsection 5.1 presents the testing methods that we have employed for the development of our strategies. Subsection 5.2 introduces an approach for improving the decision-making process of our agents. Finally, Subsect. 5.3 introduces the use of interactive programming for faster prototyping.

5.1   Unit and AB Tests for Agents

We have employed two methods to test our strategies: unit tests and an AB statistical analysis for goal-oriented tests; the combination consolidates a perspective which we call Goal-Oriented Test-Driven Development (GOTDD) [10]. For the unit tests, a preliminary testing framework was developed allowing the developer to perform special compilation process for test (e.g., by running `$./gradlew test`) which performs configured tests. This command can be run locally at any time during the development, and also it can be configured in Continuous Integration tools (e.g. GitHub actions) in order to report test errors to the developer. For explaining the unit test facility, let us consider a Jason rule for calculating the Manhattan distance between two points, as illustrated in Fig. 4.

```
distance(X1,Y1,X2,Y2,D) :-
    D = math.abs(X2-X1) + math.abs(Y2-Y1).
```

Fig. 4. Calculate the Manhattan distance between two points

In GOTDD, it is expected to have tests for every component of the system. The unit test facility runs all plans labelled as `@some_label[test]` and provides testing plans such as `assert_equals` for comparing values and `assert_true` to check if a belief exists, among others. For example, a way to test the rule `distance` is giving some coordinates in which the distance is already known, so that we can compare the answer from the rule with the known answer as shown in Fig. 5.

```
@[test]
+!testDistance :
    distance(0,0,3,3,D0) &
    distance(-30,-20,4,4,D1) &
    distance(-0,10,-9,8.9,D2) &
    distance(0.7,-17,4,-19,D3)
    <-
    !assert_equals(D0,6);
    !assert_equals(D1,58);
    !assert_equals(D2,10.1);
    !assert_equals(D3,5.3).
```

Fig. 5. Unit tests for the rule called distance

To illustrate how to test a plan for achieving a goal in common situations considering the MAPC scenario, let us consider our strategy *collectivist* in which the agent has the plan find_meeting_area/5 to find a clear area to meet another agent in order to assemble blocks. In this case, our testing agent starts importing a belief base which is a snapshot of an agent's belief base captured from a simulation, i.e., this agent believes in a set of coordinates for obstacles and other objects captured from a real MAPC situation. The plan find_meeting_area/5 expects a desired coordinate, which means it will return a near coordinate that is a clear area (i.e., there are no obstacles on these coordinates, on its adjacent positions and on the other agent's coordinates and its adjacent positions). This near coordinate can be a random coordinate because the plan will test if the desired coordinate can be used, if not, it will try random neighbors. In this case, we have chosen a particular desired coordination in which we previously know that there are solution that are in the range of 10 position of the desired coordinates. We set the test for find_meeting_area/5 plan as illustrated in Fig. 6, i.e., we should receive as an answer a coordinate equal to the desired coordinate with 10 units of tolerance for X and Y values.

```
{ include("test_walking.bb") }

@[test]
+!test_find_meeting_area
    <-
    !find_meeting_area(35,0,1,XM2,YM2);
    !assert_equals(35,XM2,10); //35 +/- 10
    !assert_equals(0,YM2,10). //0 +/- 10
```

Fig. 6. Unit tests for the plan find_meeting_area

Another facility we have developed for GOTDD is the statistical analysis of some defined events. For instance, we were interested to check after a complete simulation or set of simulations if a new version of the strategy seems to be performing better than previous versions. Statistical analysis was necessary because the simulations are stochastic, and our strategies use many random factors to make decisions.

To compare a version to its previous versions, we have stored some relevant events in a file along with information about the used strategy, version and other details according to each kind of event. Figure 7 illustrates how such data is stored by using a defined internal action which appends an event and its details to a file. In this sense, the referred internal action is called in some relevant plans of the agent, such us after submitting a task in which the agent receives from the environment the information telling if it was succeeded, or it has failed.

```
!do(submit(T),RO);
if (RO == success) {
    .save_stats("taskSubmitted",T);
} else {
    .save_stats("submitFailed",T);
}
```

Fig. 7. The body of submit_task plan in which different events are being recorded.

With the MAS storing events while running simulations, we have set a particular computer to run statistical tests. Every new version was labelled in the version control system and pulled to the testing computer. We have run a batch of at least 30 rounds of simulations for each version. This number gave a minimal statistically significant set of data for each version.

To compare versions, we have to check if the distribution of data for each comparison is normal, if so, we can apply the z-test[13] between the new version and the previous version. If a statistically significant difference can be found, we compare the average of occurrences of each event, checking if the new version is maximizing or minimizing them as expected. Note that a new version can be considered better than a previous version if it maximizes some events (such as *taskSubmitted*) and minimizes others (such as *submitFailed*).

Figure 8 illustrates a comparison between version 0.17 and 0.16 for the event *taskSubmitted*. In this particular example, the distributions present no significant difference, so that we cannot say a version is better or worse than the other[14].

---

[13] We have set to use t-test for sample sizes smaller than 30.

[14] The code and complete example for statistical tests are available at https://cleberjamaral. github.io/fastpages/comparison/jupyter/2020/11/06/agents-goal-benchmark-test.html.

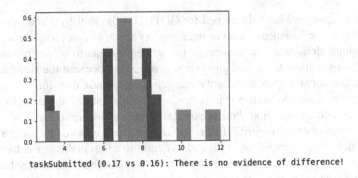

taskSubmitted (0.17 vs 0.16): There is no evidence of difference!

Fig. 8. Comparison of version 0.17 and 0.16, in this case, there is no significant difference.

With the statistical analysis, we could verify many parameters altogether. Besides *taskSubmit* and *submitFailed*, we have stored information when the agent was lost according to its beliefs and new perceptions, if the agent could not send an action to the simulation in time, among others. In this sense, in situations in which we have changed a piece of code in order to reduce the occurrence of a bug such as agent is lost, it was expected to get less of the specific bug occurrence, while other parameters were supposed to be statistically similar (or present improvement as an indirect consequence).

5.2 Reinforcement Learning with MAB

Another approach we have attempted to make use of provides tools to make dynamic choices between different agent variants at run-time, using the so-called Multi-Armed Bandit (MAB) algorithm class. MAB algorithms address a simplistic reinforcement learning problem that is concerned with the iterative choice of actions to optimize the expected reward in a stateless environment [13]. As a toy example, one may consider an agent that needs to choose which slot machine in a set she should pull (assuming not pulling a machine is no option), considering the reward history the agent has obtained from previous pulls. Thereby, the agent has to trade off exploitation (pulling the machine with the highest expected reward) and exploration ('trying out' a machine that may potentially yield a higher expected reward in the future). In the context of the contest, a MAB algorithm could have potentially been used to dynamically switch strategies within matches. A Jason extension that supports two simple MAB algorithms was implemented. However, the extension was not utilized during the contest, because no reliable assessment of its usefulness was conducted.

5.3 Interactive Programming Support

Finally, we have used interactive programming in this MAPC using *jacamo-web* IDE [2,3]. Interactive programming allows to develop a system while it is running, without stopping it. It was useful for prototyping and debugging some functions. To launch *jacamo-web* with an ordinary JaCaMo project, it is just needed to add it as a dependency. *Jacamo-web* instantiates *jacamo-rest* [1] on the backend and provides a client interface to access by a web browser. This client interface facilitates monitoring the system, understanding of which artifacts and agents are instantiated, and which agents are interacting with the elements of the environment. Besides, and most important for our purposes, it provides interface to send commands to agents and to change agent's code, allowing to hot-swap a new source code.

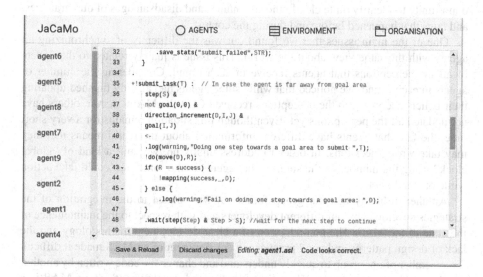

Fig. 9. Jacamo-web interface for changing a running agent's code.

To make it possible to prototype agents while running, it was necessary to make a few adaptations to MAPC server configuration and agents' code. On the MAPC server, we changed the *agentTimeout* configuration (default is 4 s) to a minute or more. We have changed on agent so that it does not send its action to the environment without a developer command. This was necessary because with the default timeout, the steps may run too fast and the developer may not have time to realize and understand what is going on in time to visualize and prototype changes when a situation asks.

To give an example of a situation in which *jacamo-web* has helped, we had some problems in which the agent got close to the right destination, but it did not realize that. In some cases, we have created beliefs and for some reason, sometimes the beliefs were not updated correctly according to agent's movements. In this case with *jacamo-web* we could check that the belief was wrong according to the agent's actual position, and we could make changes on agent's code to avoid such mistakes. The situation was used to debug and to prototype an improvement, making the development of a hot-fix much faster. Figure 9 illustrates how an agent's code can be modified and loaded on a running agent.

6 Conclusion

Participating in the MAPC, provided us – in addition to the contest results – with a series of feedback about tools and languages used during the implementation of the MAS, which allowed us to test new features and improve some aspects about them. Our final classification was not the best that we could achieve; however, we had the opportunity to identify quite clearly the advantages and disadvantages of our strategies, and bugs that happened before and during the contest.

One of the main issues that we found out was the difficulty of synchronizing all agents with the same view about the world. This issue is mainly related to the update of all the perceptions that agents receive in each round. Considering the number of agents in each round, we noticed that while some agents had already finished updating their beliefs according to the perceptions received from the MAPC server, others have not updated all the perceptions yet. Even though this situation remains for a very short time, the fact that agents have different information about the world means that they may take wrong decisions. In order to address this issue, we built a kind of "global clock" using the number of the step, so that agents in the same step could take action while others do not.

Another difficulty that our group found out was related to the integration of the strategies developed by our different developers and with respect to the maintenance of the code of the MAS. The non-adoption of a clear development methodology and the lack of design patterns and good practices in development of an MAS made it difficult for a member of our group to quickly understand and change the code written by another developer of our own group. We believe the "shared development" of an MAS is a challenging problem and we plan to address it in future projects, having as a result a set of good practices and design patterns.

A third challenge that we found out during the development of the MAS was related to debugging and testing. Testing and debugging were mostly done by means of inspecting the agent internal state (beliefs, goals, intentions, etc.) and by printed/logged messages in the terminal or files. Although these means were enough to find out some bugs in the code, they were not so suitable to test the MAS after making some changes in the code, in order to ensure that nothing was affected in other parts of the code. An assertion mechanism, named *JaCaMo Unit Tests*, was then developed by our group focused on Jason agents, so that a developer can annotate a plan with the label *@[test]* and insert assertions in its code. The plans annotated with *test* are then automatically executed in every *push of the code* into *git* and have their assertions tested. When we have a plan being tested on every push, we have the opportunity to be advised if some change has affected other parts of the MAS. It is specially effective when we have many developers working in the same project. Performing static tests may also be a more convenient and faster way to test new features. The static tests usually run faster than the simulation.

Although useful, a static test framework is not a silver bullet, in special when the scenario is stochastic. For instance, we raised a bunch of possible causes for an agent to have excessive intentions (which causes delay, possibly step loses and agent's crash). The common way to chase such a bug is simulating and monitoring some aspects of the agent and the environment (e.g. printing log messages) until occurring the error. Then, we can go backward until finding the bug. However, it is often hard to reach the specific condition in a stochastic scenario. In such cases, an AB test between the new version and previous ones was useful. It did some job of the developer by monitoring aspects and grabbing useful data in order to fix bugs. This approach also helped to prioritize our developing efforts, since we started to count how often the monitored bugs were happening.

We have not used advanced planning, machine learning[15], or similar artificial intelligence techniques, and we have neither used an explicit organization, nor norms in our team for this year, even though we have found situations where we could have benefited from some of these methods. In our future participation, depending on the new scenario, we plan, for example, to integrate both machine learning and an explicit organization in our team. While the use of machine learning can help our agents to learn more about the opponents at run-time, an explicit organization can help to improve the coordination and collaboration among the agents, besides it better separates the organization code from the agents and the environment. For example, in this latter case, all the coordination and collaboration in our current version are hard-coded in the agents' code and depend on interactions among agents. Furthermore, there are some strategies that we need to adapt in our team, such as (i) to allow the agents to accept tasks that require more than two blocks; (ii) to make the agents able to walk in the world carrying on more than four blocks; (iii) make the agents able to build more complex structures; and (iv) review our defense strategy to fix bugs that we found during the contest.

Finally, to improve the current scenario, we suggest the addition of new agent types (such as existed in scenarios of previous years), which may also bring new challenges and elevate the importance of *organizations* for agents. Some examples of agents that could be added is a repairer, which could make others enabled again, and specific types to link the type of block to the type of agent that could attach that block, which means that to attach some block an agent of certain type is required.

Short Answers

A   Team Overview: Short Answers

A.1   Participants and Their Background

What was your motivation to participate in the contest?
There are three main aims of our this year's participation: (i) improve our MAS developing skills, (ii) evaluate new features developed in the JaCaMo platform, and (iii) evaluate some proposals developed in final works of some team members, such as their thesis.

What is the history of your group? (course project, thesis, ...)
Our agent team, named JaCaMo Builders, was developed by a group formed by five PhDs, two PhD students, and two undergraduate students from different institutions: Federal University of Santa Catarina (UFSC), Federal Institute of Santa Catarina (IFSC), Santa Catarina State University (UDESC), and Umeå University. Maicon, Tiago, Cleber, and Maiquel were PhD students of prof. Jomi

---

[15] Although we have developed a Multi-Armed Bandit approach.

and worked in their thesis with MAS. The MAPC was introduced to them by Jomi and since the "Agents in Mars" scenario, at least some of them is always attending the MAPC. Nowadays, they became professors in different universities/institutes and still work with research in the MAS field. Vitor is a student of Maiquel and Robson a student of Maicon, both having a contact with MAS for the first time. Finally, Timotheus and Mauri are respectively a PhD student and a professor having a first contact with the MAPC.

What is your field of research? Which work therein is related?

Most of our group members are researchers in the MAS field, working on the development of languages, platforms, and other tools in order to bring advances in the MAS field.

For example, one of the PhD thesis, is studying an automated model for generating MAS organisations. In the context of the contest, a possible application could be on deciding an initial setup for the agents of a match. We have created different strategies which can be seen as organisational roles. In this sense, on the design time, it could produce organisational structures in which the agents are arranged in, testing which one is performing better. Another possible application could be on generating coalitions for achieving particular tasks on the running time. Unfortunately, we had no time to exploit it in this contest since we had other more important issues to solve.

A.2   Statistics

Did you start your agent team from scratch or did you build on your own or someone else's agents (e.g. from last year)?

Our team of agents was developed from scratch.

How much time did you invest in the contest (for programming, organizing your group, other)?

We started to work on the team development in April/2020 and we surely spent about 1000 h until the contest.

How was the time (roughly) distributed over the months before the contest?

We tried to work the same amount of time during all the months before the contest, however, after the first attempt of qualification we had to invest some more time to work in the building of structures. The qualification was a little harder than what we imagined and it made our group to change the priorities of which strategies we should implement first.

How many lines of code did you produce for your final agent team?

The agents' code has about 5914 lines written in the Jason language. The CArtAgO environment has about 947 lines while other Java files have about 1258 lines.

How many people were involved?

Our group is formed by nine people: five PhDs, two PhD students, and two undergraduate students from different institutions: Federal University of Santa Catarina (UFSC), Federal Institute of Santa Catarina (IFSC), Santa Catarina State University (UDESC), and Umeå University.

When did you start working on your agents?

We started to work on the team development in April/2020.

A.3 Technology and Techniques

Did you make use of agent technology/AOSE methods or tools? What were your experiences?

We used agent technology to develop a team for this year's scenario, however we did not use any software engineering method or tool during the development of our team. Part of our group of people had already previous experience in the MAPC as well as with agent oriented programming.

Agent programming languages and/or frameworks?

We adopted the JaCaMo platform to develop our team, in special, the Jason language for the agents and CArtAgO to develop the environment.

Methodologies (e.g. Prometheus)?

We did not use any methodology.

Notation (e.g. Agent UML)?

We did not use any notation.

Coordination mechanisms (e.g. protocols, games, . . .)?

We use auction to decide how agents decide who accepts which task as well as to decide which agent becomes helped to another agent. In addition, a synchronization mechanism was developed to synchronize all agents in the same world.

Other (methods/concepts/tools)?

We did not use any other special tool, method or concepts during the development of our team. However, we implemented an algorithm to schedule internal tasks that agents have to perform in certain moments.

A.4 Agent System Details

How do your agents decide what to do?

The agents have an internal scheduler to decide which tasks to perform in each moment. These tasks are not the tasks of the scenario, but the internal tasks of the agent, such as to accomplish some internal goal. In order to decide what to do (which action to take) in the MAPC scenario, it depends on what the agent is doing in the moment. For example, an agent that planned to move from a cell to another cell is following a route that was calculated in the current of previous steps. Another example is when the agents still do not share the same world map, which means the agents try to meet the other agents of the team as soon as possible.

How do your agents decide how to do it?

It all depends on what the agents want to do. If the agents are still in the beginning of the match, they use a strategy to explore the map and synchronize all the information. The information is shared among agents by means of merging the information of every two agents that meet each other. All the information is stored in an artifact and each agent has access to its own information until it meets another agent. If the agents are already working with some task, a single agent works individually if the task requires a single block and if the task requires two blocks, the agent asks another agent to bring a block and to finish the structure. Agents who have the goal to defend the goal zones and task boards try first to find these places and then get four blocks in order to carry until the goal zone or task board that it found before. The defenders observe when opponents arrive near to the task boards or goal zones that they are protecting and try to move accordingly in order to block the way of the opponents.

How does the team work together? (i.e. coordination, information sharing, ...) How decentralised is your approach?

Our team of agents in completely decentralised in the beginning of the match. During the beginning of the match, agents try to build a "common map" which is stored in an CArtAgO artifact, shared among all agents. After building the "common map", it became the only point of information about the map. All decisions are taken in a non-centralised way, however different agents may participate, for example, to build some structure together.

Do your agents make use of the following features: Planning, Learning, Organisations, Norms? If so, please elaborate briefly.

We did not use planning, learning, an explicit organisation, or norms in our team for this year, even though we plan to integrate machine learning in our team somewhere in the future.

Can your agents change their behavior during runtime? If so, what triggers the changes?

We organized a match in two main phases: the first phase is the exploration and synchronization and it aims to make all agents be in the same world. The second phase is more focused on accepting, building and submitting tasks, defending goal zones, so that, agents would not try to explore so much the map anymore. What triggers this change of behavior is when the agents fulfil enough exploration and synchronization of the map.

Did you have to make changes to the team (e.g. fix critical bugs) during the contest?

We had a critical issue happening during the transitions among different matches, however to fix such issue we simply restarted the agents.

How did you go about debugging your system? What kinds of measures could improve your debugging experience?

We used assertions (a new feature of the Jason language and also available for JaCaMo) as well as print/log messages.

During the contest you were not allowed to watch the matches. How did you understand what your team of agents was doing? Did this understanding help you to improve your team's performance?

We had a log system in our MAS, where agents often print what they are doing during the execution, such as which action they are performing, where they are and when they accept and submit some task. It was not completely precise to understand what was going on during the contest however it was enough to give some idea about how the agents were behaving.

Did you invest time in making your agents more robust? How?

Yes. We invested some time to make agents to reset themselves if they understand that they are performing bad actions (or not any action) or get lost in the world.

A.5   Scenario and Strategy

What is the main strategy of your agent team?

We considered four main problems to deal with the proposed scenario: world exploration and data synchronization; routing and walking in the world; accepting, building, and submitting tasks; and defense of the goal zones. All these "sub-problems" are important in the scenario of the MAPC 2020. Synchronization in the exploration phase is important to let all agents to see the "same world" and it allows agents to make better and faster decisions. Routing plays an important role for the team, because the scenario is quite dynamic and investing time to make the agents to walk in such a scenario may give us a good reward during the competition. We considered the acceptance, building and submission of the tasks as the core part of this MAPC scenario; once the agents needs to decide which tasks they could accept and also how to actually build a structure, because it does not depend on a single agent, but a small group of agents. Finally, as a way to also maximize our chances to perform better than other teams, agents needs to defend the goal zones with the main aim to avoid that the adversary could deliver their tasks.

Please explain whether you think you came up with a good strategy or you rather enabled your agents to find the best strategy.

We spent some time before to start writing code of our agents discussing the strategies that we would adopt in our team. In addition, we also made multiple versions of our team and made them play against each other to decide which would be the strategies that we keep for the final version of our team.

Did you implement any strategy that tries to interfere with your opponents?

In order to maximize the chances to win the contest we saw two main aspects to consider: to make as much points as possible as well as to minimize the number of points that the opponent could make. In order to minimize the number of points that the opponent could make, we adopted a strategy where some agents had the goal to avoid that opponent agents could approach the goal zones or task boards, so that, the opponent agents could not make as much points as they wanted.

How do your agents decide which tasks to complete?

Once the agents know at least a task board and a goal zone to submit a task, the agents can start accepting tasks. They often accepted tasks with single blocks, however in some situations they also could accept tasks of at a maximum of two blocks. We did not try to accept tasks that require more than two blocks once the organization of the agents would me much more complex, and we focused in other aspects of the scenario instead.

How do your agents coordinate assembling and delivering a structure for a task?

We do not define a priori which agents will form each group to complete a task. The decision of which agent will help to accomplish each task is made by means of a kind of auction with the available agents in the moment. In addition, some agents may accomplish tasks individually, when the tasks is formed by a single block.

Which aspect(s) of the scenario did you find particularly challenging?

The characteristics of the map were the most challenging aspects for our group, such as the "infinity" map and the fact that agents do not know who they are seeing in the map.

A.6   And the Moral of It Is ...

What did you learn from participating in the contest?

Participating in the contests is always a great challenge and even though several members of our team participated in more than two editions we always have a lot of new things to learn. This year scenario was a lot more challenging and brought problems that demanded a precise coordination of the agents, such as to build a structure and to explore and synchronise the map. This new challenged allowed us to elaborate and test different strategies to make agents collaborate in order to build strategies and also to minimize the time that agents take to be situated in a common world.

What advice would you give to yourself before the contest/another team wanting to participate in the next?

Our main advice is to build a team as simple as possible in order to minimize bugs and complexity of the agents in a first moment. After having a first simple version of the team fully working, increment it with more complex strategies and test it before to move forward to new strategies.

What are the strong and weak points of your team?

The main strength of our teams is that agents do not only focus on accepting, building and submitting tasks to get rewards, but also to defend the goal zones and task boards to prevent that the adversary gets rewards. So, our expectation was to maximize our chances to get a bigger score than our adversaries.

The main weaknesses of our agents is that they have a little difficulty to move when carrying more blocks, which can make it difficult for an agent that is holding a more complex structure to escape the clearing area when some clear action happens or to move around in areas with too many obstacles. In addition, our agents do not commit to tasks that demand more than two blocks, which can be a clear disadvantage in scenarios with few tasks that demand no more than two blocks. We did not spend so much time on improving it once we tried to make our agents build the structures near to the goal zones.

Where did you benefit from your chosen programming language, methodology, tools, and algorithms?

The choice for the JaCaMo platform to develop our team of agents was an important point for our group. The separation of the MAS implementation according to different first-class abstractions such as organization, agents, and environment made it easier for us to organize and maintain the code of the MAS. In addition, several members of our group had already some experience with the JaCaMo platform.

Which problems did you encounter because of your chosen technologies?

The main problem that we found in our chosen technologies was the difficulty to debug the execution, so that, we implemented a feature based on "asserts" to help us to identify some wrong behaviors in the system, as well as print messages.

Did you encounter new problems during the contest?

We found a problem during the transitions between matches, which did not happen during our local tests. In addition, we noticed some issues when agents needed to submit tasks of two blocks and defend task boards and goal zones to prevent the opponent agents to complete their tasks.

Did playing against other agent teams bring about new insights on your own agents?

Yes. We noticed during the contest that most teams looked not so ready for the situation in which the task boards or goal zones were occupied by some opponent agent and such opponent agent not allowing the agents to freely submit tasks or get blocks. However, unfortunately, our strategy to defend the task boards and goal zones did not work well during the contest.

What would you improve (wrt. your agents) if you wanted to participate in the same contest a week from now (or next year)?

We would have a couple of issues to fix in order to make our team perform better during that week, such as (1) improve the transition between the matches, (2) fix some problems when agents commit to tasks of two blocks, (3) fix some problems in our defender agents (the ones that try to block the access of the opponent agents to the goal zones and task boards).

Which aspect of your team cost you the most time?

We feel that the most challenging aspect of the implementation of our team of agents was the map exploration and map synchronization, which played an important role in all other things that agents could do. So that, making the agents discover the dimensions of the map and setting all agents in the "same map" took us a plenty of time. In addition, we spent quite a huge time in debugging the system in order to fix some problems during the agents' execution.

What can be improved regarding the contest/scenario for next year?

We suggest the inclusion of new agent types (such as existed in scenarios of previous years), which may also bring new challenges and stress the organization of agents. For example, some blocks could be brought just by certain type of agent.

In addition, we also suggest to keep the scenario of this year's scenario for the next edition of the contest, without big changes. As a first time attending the contest for this scenario, we devoted a huge amount of time to implement the team and we see a lot yet possible to improve in the team. During the contest, we noticed other teams also demonstrated some issues that could be fixed for the next edition. Thus, our suggestion is to try to keep the next edition's scenario as close as possible to this edition.

Why did your team perform as it did? Why did the other teams perform better/worse than you did?

We believe some of our strategies were a little buggy during the contests, such as the submission of tasks of two blocks and the defense of task boards and goal zones. These two strategies play a very important role in our team and if they do not work properly the team becomes a lot weaker than it really is. In addition, we had a serious problem during transitions between matches, which made us to restart the full MAS during the contest. It means, our agents lost all their beliefs, goals and knowledge about the world where they were situated.

If you participated in the "free-for-all" event after the contest, did you learn anything new about your agents from that?

In the "free-for-all", our team seemed to perform better, and we held the third place among four participants. Our team was able to submit three tasks of single blocks however another team did not submit any task. We also observed that several agents (of different teams) were occupying the goal zones most of the time, which made it more difficult for the teams to submit tasks.

References

1. Amaral, C.J., Hübner, J.F., Kampik, T.: A resource-oriented abstraction for managing multi-agent systems. Towards jacamo-rest (2020)
2. Amaral, C.J., Hübner, J.F.: Jacamo-web is on the fly: an interactive multi-agent system IDE. In: Dennis, L.A., Bordini, R.H., Lespérance, Y. (eds.) EMAS 2019. LNCS (LNAI), vol. 12058, pp. 246–255. Springer, Cham (2020). https://doi.org/10.1007/978-3-030-51417-4_13
3. Amaral, C.J., Kampik, T., Cranefield, S.: A framework for collaborative and interactive agent-oriented developer operations. In: Proceedings of the 19th International Conference on Autonomous Agents and MultiAgent Systems, AAMAS 2020, Richland, SC, pp. 2092–2094. International Foundation for Autonomous Agents and Multiagent Systems (2020)
4. Behrens, T.M., Hindriks, K.V., Dix, J.: Towards an environment interface standard for agent platforms. Ann. Math. Artif. Intell. **61**(4), 261–295 (2011)
5. Boissier, O., Bordini, R., Hübner, J.F., Ricci, A., Santi, A.: Multi-agent oriented programming with JaCaMo. Sci. Comput. Program. **78**(6), 747–761 (2013)
6. Boissier, O., Bordini, R.H., Hubner, J., Ricci, A.: Multi-Agent Oriented Programming: Programming Multi-Agent Systems Using JaCaMo. MIT Press, Cambridge (2020)
7. Bordini, R.H., Wooldridge, M., Hübner, J.F.: Programming Multi-Agent Systems in AgentSpeak Using Jason. Wiley, Hoboken (2007)
8. Gabriely, Y., Rimon, E.: Spanning-tree based coverage of continuous areas by a mobile robot. In: Proceedings 2001 ICRA. IEEE International Conference on Robotics and Automation, vol. 2, pp. 1927–1933 (2001)
9. Hübner, J.F., Sichman, J.S., Boissier, O.: Developing organised multi-agent systems using the MOISE+ model: programming issues at the system and agent levels. Int. J. Agent-Oriented Softw. Eng. **1**(3/4), 370–395 (2007)
10. Kampik, T., Amaral, C.J., Hübner, J.F.: Developer operations and engineering multi-agent systems (2021)
11. Köster, M., Schlesinger, F., Dix, J.: The multi-agent programming contest 2012. In: Dastani, M., Hübner, J.F., Logan, B. (eds.) ProMAS 2012. LNCS (LNAI), vol. 7837, pp. 174–195. Springer, Heidelberg (2013). https://doi.org/10.1007/978-3-642-38700-5_11

12. Ricci, A., Piunti, M., Viroli, M.: Environment programming in multi-agent systems: an artifact-based perspective. AAMAS **23**, 158–192 (2011). https://doi.org/10.1007/s10458-010-9140-7

13. Vermorel, J., Mohri, M.: Multi-armed bandit algorithms and empirical evaluation. In: Gama, J., Camacho, R., Brazdil, P.B., Jorge, A.M., Torgo, L. (eds.) ECML 2005. LNCS (LNAI), vol. 3720, pp. 437–448. Springer, Heidelberg (2005). https://doi.org/10.1007/11564096_42

Author Index

Printed in the United States
by Baker & Taylor Publisher Services